W9-BDE-665

LIVING THE DISCIPLINE

# Living the Discipline

United Methodist Theological Reflections
on War, Civilization, and Holiness

D. Stephen Long

WILLIAM B. EERDMANS PUBLISHING COMPANY
GRAND RAPIDS, MICHIGAN

Copyright © 1992 by Wm. B. Eerdmans Publishing Co.

255 Jefferson Ave. S.E., Grand Rapids, Mich. 49503

All rights reserved

Printed in the United States of America

**Library of Congress Cataloging-in-Publication Data**

Long, D. Stephen, 1960-
   Living the discipline: United Methodist theological reflections on war,
civilization, and holiness / D. Stephen Long.
      p.      cm.
   Includes bibliographical references and index.
   ISBN  0-8028-0634-1 (pbk.)
      1. Pacifism — Religious aspects — United Methodist Church (U.S.)
2. Christianity and culture. 3. Holiness. 4. United Methodist Church
(U.S.) — Doctrines. 5. United Methodist Church (U.S.) — Membership.
6. Methodist Church — Doctrines. 7. Methodist Church — Membership.
8. United States — Moral conditions. I. Title.
BX8382.2.Z5L66  1992
261.8'73 — dc20                                             92-18048
                                                                      CIP

*For Ricka,*
*whose hospitality*
*turns strangers*
*into friends*

# Contents

# Preface

I began writing this book before the Gulf War and finished shortly after the end of the war. As I write this preface, the United States government has sent troops into Los Angeles to quell the riots that began after the innocent verdict in the Rodney King case. If ever there were need for a peaceable people who refuse to use violence, and yet also seek to speak truthfully and honestly, it is now (as it was yesterday, and the day before . . . ). The United Methodist Church holds up peaceableness as the norm for all of its members; yet in its comfortable accommodation with the United States of America, it has refused to call its members to accountability. This book is written with the hope that it will initiate a discussion within the life of United Methodism and Protestant Christianity, for we need to recover a sense of disciplined Christian living that calls people out of the violence of the everyday.

I could only write this book because of friends who seek to keep me accountable to the best within my own tradition. Thus I owe a great debt of gratitude to the ecumenical prayer group that has met in my home over the past three years. We have prayed, worked, and struggled together over what it means to be the church, often testing the limits of our own peaceableness, but always willing to be reconciled. Many of the ideas I have used here developed directly from our prayers together.

I also need to thank Fritz Bauerschmidt, Claire Clyburn, Stanley Hauerwas, and Brent Laytham for reading through the following material and making helpful comments. It is customary at this point in a preface to thank such people for all their good insights, and yet release them from all possible errors. I consider that a false sign of heroism which I do not want to embody. If anything good comes from this book, they need to be especially thanked. If anything negative arises, they are good enough friends to stand with me. Thus, I thank them.

I also want to thank Andrea Gansle for allowing me to include her application for conscientious objector status in this book. Her application was originally denied by the U.S. Air Force and is currently under appeal.

Finally, let me thank William B. Eerdmans Publishing Company for its willingness to publish this book, and Jennifer Hoffman for her editorial assistance.

# Introduction: A Pacifist Prolegomenon

Is the United Methodist Church pacifist? Constitutionally we are; practically we are not. Since 1968, pacifism has been our constitutional stance. Article 16 of the Confession of Faith in our constitution states:

> We believe civil government derives its just powers from the sovereign God. As Christians we recognize the government under whose protection we reside and believe such governments should be based on, and be responsible for, the recognition of human rights under God. *We believe war and bloodshed are contrary to the gospel and spirit of Christ.* We believe it is the duty of Christian citizens to give moral strength and purpose to their respective governments through sober, righteous, and godly living.[1]

1. Article 16 of our Confession of Faith, par. 68 in *The Book of Discipline of the United Methodist Church* (Nashville: The Methodist Publishing House, 1988); emphasis added. This edition of the *Discipline* is cited throughout, unless otherwise noted.
   That Article 16 is pacifist is not obviously self-evident. However, placed in its historical context (as will be done in Chapter 2), placed in a Wesleyan doctrine of sanctification, and compared with a similar Article of Religion of the Anglican Church, it does become obvious that Article 16 commits United Methodism to a normatively pacifist stance. Moreover, language similar to that of Article 16 is used by the United Methodist Church to prohibit homosexual activity (see the *Book of Discipline*, p. 96), which only provides further warrant that any consistent reading of Article 16 commits the United Methodist Church to pacifism.

1

This article cannot be changed unless a three-fourths majority of the members of the annual and missionary conferences present at a General Conference vote to do so. This article is binding on all United Methodists, and pastors and laity are charged with not disseminating any doctrine on war contrary to this article.[2]

Pastors are also charged in the United Methodist *Discipline* with "counseling members of the Church and the community concerning military service and its alternatives."[3] United Methodism claims to be a pacifist church and requires pastors to counsel members concerning military service, yet in practice United Methodism is *not* a pacifist church. The central purpose of this book is to argue that United Methodist pastors should counsel their parishioners to be pacifists.

If upon hearing that pacifism is the church's legally binding stance, the United Methodists responded as the Israelites did under Josiah's reforms when the law was recovered (see 2 Chron. 34–35), I could simply quote the *Discipline* and expect the United Methodist people to repent and to begin to keep this law. However, such expectations I do not have. Thus to fulfill the central purpose of this book two other subordinate themes are necessary. On the one hand, I need to provide a theological foundation for pacifism that will be convincing to all believers who take their baptismal vows seriously. On the other hand, I must explain convincingly how the United Methodists came to a point where their constitutional stance and their practice are in direct contradiction. These two themes support each other. Methodism suffers because of a poor theological foundation that accepts such contradictory statements as "war is incompatible with the example and teaching of Christ, yet Christians can participate in

2. See par. 2621 in the *Book of Discipline*, where "dissemination of doctrines contrary to the established standards of doctrine of the Church" is described as a charge warranting a trial for both laity and pastors. Article 16 above is an "established standard of doctrine of the Church" and is therefore legally binding.

3. Par. 439.i in the *Book of Discipline*.

war." Exposing the reasons for this poor theological foundation and providing a different theological foundation will set us well on the way to fulfilling the central purpose of this book.

At the present time, Methodism faces the peculiar irony that pastors who would actually counsel their parishioners in accordance with the constitutional stance of the church would soon be marginalized. Counseling people against war is a risky business. Members could leave churches, and pastors are evaluated mainly on the basis of membership. Therefore, if you uphold the position of the United Methodist Church on war, there is little place for you within United Methodism. How did we arrive at such a strange contradiction? To answer this question, I must tell a story of theology in America.


## LIVING OR ADJUSTING THE DISCIPLINE?

Often the claim is made that in the nineteenth century the Methodists lost a sense of discipline. I disagree. The Methodists did not lose their discipline; instead, the purpose of their discipline shifted from holiness of heart and life to being relevant to American culture. Even today, relevance to American culture remains a rigid and unquestioned form of discipline within Methodism. This form of disciplining members has a long tradition in American Methodism.

Since the inception of the Methodist Church in 1784, Methodist leaders often sought to bring reform through adjusting the *Discipline* of the church to accommodate the wider culture. "Culture" or "civilization" (the two terms were used interchangeably) became a foundational standard for our self-identity. We identified ourselves as a people capable of being "practical," a term that became synonymous with flexibility and openness to the wider culture. Whether the culture was frontier America or newly developing city life, Methodists un-

3

derstood their task as being practically "relevant" to that "culture." Of course, relevance is important, but our desire to be "culturally" relevant has prohibited theological reflection. We find ourselves constantly in the position of defining culture(s) first, and then bringing in theology at a secondary level to address that predefined "culture."

In the second half of the nineteenth century, "civilization" explicitly provided a foundation for Methodist theology. Both conservative theologians such as Nathan Bangs and liberal theologians such as Borden Parker Bowne understood American culture to be the context for Methodist theology. Once American culture was adopted as the primary context for theology, Methodist theology departed from Wesley, Asbury, and the early Methodist women and men who established the church. The church's foundational documents, drawn from the community of faith, were replaced by documents drawn from American culture.[4]

Once this transition was made, secular notions of "freedom of conscience," "pragmatist reasoning," "civilization," and "relevance to culture" created a monolithic dogmatism within Methodism. One reason why the United Methodist Church claims to be pacifist and yet marginalizes pacifists is that the church's constitutionally binding foundational documents were replaced by these secular notions in the practical functioning and theological reflection of the church. Therefore, our "theology" arises from American culture rather than from Scripture and church tradition.

The centrality of the American cultural context for theology is reflected in the curricula in our seminaries. Seminaries remain the central formative theological influence on pastors. In the 1860s at Grinnell College in Iowa a new discipline was created

4. Francis Asbury explicitly repudiated any attempt to portray Methodism's success as its ability to be relevant to American culture. See his "Valedictory Address," in *Wesleyan Theology: A Sourcebook*, ed. Thomas A. Langford (Durham, NC: Labyrinth Press, 1984), pp. 67-85.

within theological education known as "applied Christianity." The purpose of the new discipline was to begin with the best current sociological science, allow sociology to read and interpret the needs of culture, and then apply Christianity to those needs. The discipline of "applied Christianity" represented a more general movement within theological education. Theological educators allowed psychology to define how pastors counsel, ethics and moral philosophy to define the Christian moral life, economics to define church polity, philosophy to structure systematic theology, literary and historical criticism to tell us how Scripture can be read, etc. The art of theology as the "queen of the sciences" — utilizing all forms of knowledge but interpreting that knowledge through Scripture and church tradition — was lost. Theology itself became marginalized as an educational system developed that was predominantly concerned with disciplining pastors so that they would be relevant to the wider culture.

This new form of discipline was successful. The United Methodist Church is now so relevant to American culture that little difference between the church and the wider culture can be found; thus we are losing members out of apathy. Why be passionate about a church that can hardly be distinguished from the wider culture?

## THE PROBLEM WITH "CULTURE"

The general movement of applying Christianity to culture creates three problems for theology. First, it too easily assumes that "culture" can be understood before theology is invoked. Second, it assumes that "culture" exists as something in itself. Third, it marginalizes the role of theology within theological education and refuses to see that Christianity is itself a culture, with the art of theology as its primary form of self-critical reflection.

If "culture" is defined by disciplines other than theology *before* theology is brought to bear, then the world that is presented to us will lack traditional theological categories such as sin and redemption, prevenient grace, and the place of Christ as the foundation of and purpose for creation.

Let me give an example to explain this. If we allow the biologist to define the "natural order" for us, then the biologist will tell us that the relationship between lions and lambs is simply a part of the food chain. Lions *naturally* eat lambs because of the instinct of self-preservation. The food chain is an amoral fact of nature; it is simply the way things are. But any theologian with knowledge of Scripture and church tradition would realize that this description of the "natural order" is unacceptable. This relationship between lions and lambs is not "natural"; it is a sign of a disordered creation rebelling against the harmony and peace that defines its Creator.

In the kingdom of God, lions and lambs lie down together. That kingdom is visibly present in Christ, who is described as the "Lamb who was slain" as well as the "Lion of the tribe of Judah" (Rev. 5:5, 12). This understanding of the relationship between lions and lambs qualifies the biologist's interpretation, which views the "natural" instinct of self-preservation as a self-evident fact that can be known by observing the behavior of lions and lambs. The theological interpretation may make no difference in our expectations of the behavior of lions and lambs, but it does make a difference for how we define our world and for our expectations within that world. Those expectations will be lost if we allow biologists alone to define the wider culture to which we then apply Christianity.

Not only is the general understanding of theological education rendered problematic because it allows culture to be defined pre-theologically; it is also problematic because it assumes that we know what "culture" is. As Raymond Williams — one of the originators of cultural criticism — reminds us, *culture* is "one of the two or three most complicated words in the English language."[5] *Culture* was originally a "noun of process" that meant the tending and harvesting of crops. It was first generally used to describe the tending and development of people in the early part of the sixteenth century. In the middle of the eighteenth century, *culture* became synonymous with *civilization*. Many Western European philosophers assumed that their "culture" had progressed to a stage that was the culmination of the tending and development process, resulting in civilization. They believed that their forms of government and their life-style represented a "cultured" and "civilized" people — the development process was complete, and the next step was to extend the process to the "uncultured" and "uncivilized."

In the late eighteenth century, philosopher Johann Gottfried von Herder challenged the equation of culture with civilization. He wrote:

> Men of all the quarters of the globe, who have perished over the ages, you have not lived solely to manure the earth with your ashes, so that at the end of time your posterity should be made happy by European culture. The very thought of a superior European culture is a blatant insult to the majesty of Nature.[6]

The challenge Herder and other critical theorists after him offered to the idea of culture severed the connection between Western European civilization and "culture" and opened up the possibility of speaking of "cultures" rather than "culture." This led to a dramatic shift in knowledge during the past one hundred years, and our educational institutions are still trying to respond to it.

Culture as "civilization" preoccupied theology in the nineteenth century. The attempt to be relevant to culture meant

5. Raymond Williams, *Keywords* (New York: Oxford University Press, 1983), p. 87.
6. Cited in ibid., p. 89.

7

that theology was accommodated to this state of "civilization."
"Civilization" actually became a foundational standard within
liberal Protestant theology. Ironically, theological education has
experienced few decisive shifts in method since the nineteenth
century. Liberal theological education still works with the basic
assumption that the purpose of Christian theology is to be
relevant to culture — except that now we understand culture
as "cultures." Thus we have a proliferation of theologies seeking to be relevant to various cultures.

Womanist, feminist, Native American, African American,
and liberation theologies often do not represent any new method
of theological reflection. They do represent a new understanding
of "culture," but insofar as they make a particular people's culture
primary and then apply Christianity after the articulation of that
culture, they betray their indebtedness to the inheritance left by
the liberal Protestant theologians of the nineteenth century.

This inheritance, articulated by Adolph von Harnack, is
the application of an essentialized Christianity to particular
cultures. He suggested that

> There are only two possibilities here: either the Gospel is in
> all respects identical with its earliest form in which case it
> came with its time and has departed with it; or else it contains
> something which, under differing historical forms, is of per-
> manent validity. The latter is the true view.[7]

Harnack sets the limits for how standard Protestant theology
is done. Either the gospel departed with the first century, or we
must look beneath cultures to find the "kernel" of Christianity
that is of "permanent validity." Thus he essentializes Christianity by refusing to place it within history and culture. When-
ever we assume that Christianity can escape its particular historical manifestation and be relevant to any culture, we accept

7. Adolph von Harnack, *What Is Christianity?* trans. Thomas Bailey
Saunders (Gloucester, MA: Peter Smith, 1978), pp. 13-14.

Harnack's terms. Harnack's project is expanded by the current proliferation of cultural theologies. They should be affirmed and embraced for the powerful way in which they challenge our understanding of "culture," but they should not be viewed as offering a substantive theological innovation.

If the purpose of Christianity is to apply the "unchanging essence" of Christianity to cultures, then we should endorse and celebrate the current proliferation of theologies. Yet other philosophies are much more adequate in providing resources to augment cultural particularities. Christianity does not fit this function well because Christianity is not in fact some unchanging essence that can be applied to various cultures and embodied in differing cultural manifestations. Christianity *is* a culture, a cultivating process that produces people in a particular way.

A central product of this cultivating process is peaceableness. The cultivating character of Christianity was understood well by early church theologians such as Justin Martyr and Tertullian, as well as by the founder of Methodism, John Wesley. Both Justin and Tertullian appropriated the Scriptural language of "swords into ploughshares" and used this language to develop a notion of a Christian culture. Justin writes:

> we who had been filled with war and mutual slaughter and every wickedness, have each one — all the world over — changed the instruments of war, the swords into ploughs and the spears into farming instruments, and we cultivate piety, righteousness, love for men, faith, and the hope which is from the Father Himself through the Crucified One.[8]

Justin recognizes that ploughs are for "culturing," and he uses this imagery to show how our participation in Christ's obedience allows us to be part of a new culture that exists "all the world over" and that is cultivated because the implements of

8. Cited in C. John Cadoux, *The Early Christian Attitude to War* (New York: Seabury Press, 1982), p. 61.

war have been broken on the cross and replaced by the implements of a new cultural movement.

These ploughshares that are formed from swords now cultivate a particular life for us, a life that creates in us certain virtues reflecting our participation in God. God as Trinity is a sociality of peaceableness.[9] Participation in the Trinity is the purpose of all creation because salvation is participation in God's own being. The obedience of the Son, as well as the ongoing work of the Holy Spirit, draws us as a church into the very life of God, a life characterized by peaceableness. Salvation is the process of the cultivation of holiness in our communal life.

Salvation as the cultivation of holiness is the subject of Wesley's most famous sermon on the doctrine of holiness, "The Circumcision of the Heart." The Spirit cultivates in Christians the "holy tempers" of humility, faith, hope, and love. These "tempers" represent a distinct Christian culture that is necessary for faithful Christian discipleship. As we shall see in the next chapter, this distinct culture often comes into conflict with the wider culture and thus cannot be assumed always to be relevant to it. Therefore, to begin theological reflection by assuming that the task of theology is to be relevant to culture challenges the distinctiveness of the Spirit's cultivating process.

Rather than understanding the theological task as seeking to be relevant to culture, we must affirm the understanding of Christianity as a culture in itself. Viewing Christianity as a culture in itself requires an explicit theology of cultivation or discipline that will seek to inculcate specific virtues or "holy tempers" in believers. One central virtue is the virtue of peaceableness. The practice of peace should be a result of the discipline of the United Methodist Church.

"Living the discipline" instead of "adjusting the discipline" requires that Methodists take seriously our official stance as a peace church, rather than seeking to interpret it away in an effort

9. See John Milbank, *Theology and Social Theory: Beyond Secular Reason* (Cambridge, MA: Basil Blackwell, 1990).

to be relevant. Counseling people concerning military service and its alternatives must become an important responsibility of the United Methodist pastorate if we are to be faithful to our heritage. For this to happen, two things need to take place. First, we must recover the art of theology itself. Second, within the art of theology we must recover the genius of Methodist theology, a theology of discipline rooted in practical divinity.

## RECOVERY OF THEOLOGY

Before we can reclaim a theology of discipline, the art of theology itself needs to be reclaimed. We are a church that suffers from a theological void. This is due in part to the fact that our theologians primarily do theology only for other theologians in the academy and fail to speak to the church. This creates a theological void in the church that is filled by trendy market practices rather than by a theology that builds on the faithfulness of those who came before us. My annual conference recently sent out a flyer that asked the question, "Are you tradition bound or market driven?" The implication of the flyer was that the "progressive" thing to be was the latter. To be market driven is to structure the church on the basis of "supply-side" ecclesiology, which begins by asking what needs exist in the wider culture and how we can meet those needs. It seeks to be relevant to American culture in the same way that IBM or General Motors does. It lifts up bureaucratic managers as the paradigm for ministry.

A supply-side ecclesiology stands in direct opposition to a theology of discipline, for the latter assumes that needs and desires need to be restructured, while the former simply accepts needs and desires as they are without asking from whence they came. We will not be able to stand against the trend toward a supply-side ecclesiology as long as the widespread theological illiteracy and fragmentation of our church remain.

At my second annual conference I spoke against a petition

on the floor. A devout layperson sitting next to me spoke in favor of the petition. After the debate was over, the layperson approached me and discussed our debate. I told him that I spoke against the petition because I thought it threatened our Wesleyan theology of the ministry. He responded, "Don't give me theology, give me Jesus." I find this layperson's response typical — and understandable — among a majority of our laity as well as many of our pastors. Methodist laity and clergy are fearful of "theology." They are fearful because theology involves a foreign language. Words such as *soteriology, Christology, pneumatology, epistemology,* and *ontology* tend to alienate people rather quickly, and for good reasons.

One reason for this alienation is that words such as these seem to shroud the mysteries of faith in a language accessible only to an academic elite. Undoubtedly, theological language is often used to create ambiguity and allow theologians to do their work in an environment free from church constraints. This reminds me of my favorite piece of graffiti, found in the restroom in the basement of Duke Divinity School's library:

> Jesus turned to his disciples and said, "Who do people say that I am?" Peter responded, "Thou art the eschatological manifestation of the ultimate ground of our being." Jesus turned to Peter and said, "Say what?!"

Perhaps the church has a place for those who discuss the merits of Jesus in terms of "the eschatological manifestation of the ultimate ground of our being," but if this becomes the primary way we speak, how can we expect laypeople to respond in any way other than "Don't give me theology, give me Jesus!"

When theology becomes so disconnected from the life of the church that only an intellectual elite are privileged to understand theological language, then both the church and theology suffer. The church suffers because it loses the critical analysis theology brings. Theology suffers because it loses its primary purpose — reflection on the life of the church by all of those who make up the church. We are all responsible for assessing how well we are traveling on the journey from sin to holiness. If this reflection does not take place corporately, or if this reflection is done in such a way that only an elite have access to it, then a theological void takes root in the church's life that allows the intellectual expression of the church to be "like a wave of the sea that is driven and tossed by the wind" (James 1:6).

If theology is to be recovered, then two things must occur. First, theology must be understood not as an incidental aspect of the faith but as a necessary part of it. Faith must be communicated, and theology is a central way in which this communication of the faith takes place. And second, theology must be made available, in one way or another, to all people.

## A UNITED METHODIST THEOLOGY OF DISCIPLINE

Recovering theology in general, however, is insufficient. Methodism has a distinctive contribution to make to the church universal in its theological understanding of the notion of "discipline." But a theology of discipline will not only be a valuable ecumenical contribution; it will also enable us to claim our pacifist stance in a way that makes our *Discipline's* statements against war intelligible.

A theology of discipline was Methodism's early genius. The polity and theology of the early Methodist movement was built on a theological position that emphasized discipline. If our vision is to shift from adjusting the discipline to living it, then we will need to reclaim this specific understanding of theology.[10]

10. The term *discipline* frightens many people because it conjures up images of inquisitional practices, paternalistic "care," and authoritarian power. This book seeks to recover "discipline" as a useful theological

The *Book of Discipline* makes our theology available to all people called Methodists. It is not a bureaucratic handbook; rather, it contains the doctrines, social stances, and church order that have been passed on from faithful Christians who preceded us. We believe the *Discipline* assists us in our present historical situation to respond faithfully on the journey from sin to holiness. Central to these doctrines and social stances is Holy Scripture, which is primary for Methodist theological reflection. Our corporate life must be bound by the Scripture in word, in deed, and in church order. Anyone who refuses to be bound by Scripture cannot be faithful to her or his baptismal vows. In our statements on war, we find the *Discipline* referring to Scripture as the central source for our theological reflection: "War is contrary to the teaching and example of Christ." Thus the *Discipline* seeks to direct the witness of Scripture to all aspects of our lives.

Before we can be called to accountability as a church for our pacifist stance, we need to reclaim the distinctive characteristic of a theology of discipline. A contribution to this process is made in Chapter 1, "Practical Divinity," by recovering a

---

category without underwriting inquisitional practices. Methodists have no choice but to claim discipline as a theological category; after all, we are supposedly bound by a *Book of Discipline*. But the recovery of a theology of discipline is necessary for a greater reason than simply that discipline is part of our heritage. The argument that follows claims that our current suspicion of discipline actually supports an insidious type of discipline that is evil because it goes unnamed. We do "discipline" our members into certain practices that bind us together, but we do so under the pretense of being "tolerant," "open," or "pluralistic," and thus we do not even realize the "disciplines" that produce Methodists in certain ways. Of course, anyone who has read post-modernist critical studies will immediately be alarmed at recent uses of the term *discipline*. Foucault's *Discipline and Punish* (New York: Vintage Books, 1979) details how discipline is used to create an unnamed, hegemonic power that goes unchallenged because it is internalized. The theology of discipline that we must incorporate into our ecclesial life should not seek to internalize a hegemonic power; rather, it should offer a "counter-discipline" to the disciplining into Western civilization that our church presently offers.

theological genre necessary for a proper theology of discipline. Practical divinity is parish-centered theology that requires communities to be capable of penitential practices, drawing upon the resources of Scripture and tradition as the rules by which they live. This chapter title also explains the genre of this book, for all that follows seeks to be an exercise in practical divinity.

While the first step in reclaiming our pacifist stance emphasizes the importance of theology for parish life, the second step narrates more fully how the secular notions obtained from our American cultural context created a rigid dogmatism and a form of "discipline" that is contrary to a proper Christian discipline. This secular form of discipline is examined in Chapter 2, "To Discipline or to Civilize." The title of this chapter suggests that Methodism in the twentieth century has been more committed to disciplining people into "Western civilization" than into holiness of heart and life. This chapter also explains the theological reason for the contradiction between the Methodist constitutional stance against war and its practice of supporting war.

After discussing the theology of discipline as the distinctive characteristic of Methodist theology and explaining how that distinctive characteristic was displaced by a doctrine of civilization, Chapter 3, "A Wesleyan Social Gospel," develops the particulars of a theology of discipline. The "law" is viewed as a gracious gift that assists us in going on to perfection, disciplining us so that we participate ever more fully in the Divine Life itself. Once this is accomplished, then the various rules and church legislation concerning war within United Methodism can be viewed as a gracious gift that is given to us by God through the church.

Only in the fourth chapter, "Counseling as a Practice of Reconciliation," and in the conclusion can we address directly how pastors can fulfill the mandate "to counsel members of the church and community concerning military service and its alternatives." Direct discussion of war and peace is neglected

15

until the end of the book because of the importance of establishing strong links between our discussion of pacifism and the theological issues discussed in the earlier chapters. "Pacifism" is too often viewed as a "social" rather than a theological concern. My argument is that United Methodists should seek to live out their discipline concerning war, not because it is the socially or politically correct thing to do, but because it makes good theological sense of who they are. The mandate should be seen as a gracious possibility for cultivating holiness.

This brings me to a final necessary component of this book that cannot be found within its covers. This book seeks to be a handbook for pastors that makes a reasoned argument based upon Scripture, Christian tradition, and parish experience. It does not seek to establish a supreme principle that is to be applied in a rigid deductive manner; rather, it seeks to engage people in a discussion. Therefore an essential component of this handbook is the practical wisdom that comes from those who work and live within the flow of parish life. The sole purpose of this handbook is to create an argument about peace and war grounded in an adequate theological expression of United Methodism. Pastors and others will need to correct what is lacking in this book; having been challenged by its argument, they will need to interpret and translate it for parish life. In essence, I am asking you to rewrite this book by engaging your people in the argument. This is what tradition is — an ongoing historical argument about who we are and what activities best express our identity.[11] I have come to the conclusion that being a peaceable people best expresses our identity. I invite you to argue with my conclusion. Hopefully the argument will allow all of us to be more faithful and to understand more fully what it means to be a people called Methodist.

11. See Alasdair MacIntyre, *After Virtue: A Study in Moral Theory,* 2nd ed. (Notre Dame: University of Notre Dame Press, 1984).

# CHAPTER ONE

## *Practical Divinity*

Methodism's distinctive theological characteristic is practical divinity. However, exactly what "practical divinity" means is a matter of debate. I understand practical divinity to consist of three characteristics: (1) a theology accessible to all Methodist people marks its style and content; (2) the story of the holiness of faithful Christian people defines its purpose; and (3) English casuistical divinity, along with the class meeting as a penitential exercise, defines more narrowly its specific shape.[1]

From these three characteristics you could surmise that this understanding of practical divinity is no longer a main element in United Methodist church life. I would agree. My intention in this chapter is to convince you of the importance of practical divinity and to provide a foundation that will make the *Book of Discipline* an important theological tool for parish life.

---

1. The introduction of the term *casuistical* requires some explanation. "Casuistry" was an important discipline in early Anglican practical divinity. Casuistry is often defined as an ethic of principles, in which the principles are used to solve problems of conscience that people confront. While that is an appropriate description, much more is needed to understand the importance of the lost art of "casuistry." The discussion in this chapter and in Chapter 4 seeks to give a fuller account of casuistry.

17

## TWENTIETH-CENTURY USAGE OF
## PRACTICAL DIVINITY

We are indebted to Professor Thomas Langford for reclaiming the phrase "practical divinity" in his book by the same title. Tradition plays an important role in Langford's discussion. He writes: "A tradition is a stream through history. A stream may have neat clear banks, or it may flow across boundaries and be difficult to trace." Langford sees the various elements of Wesleyan theology as forming a kind of "dominant current" that flows through tradition. He claims that this "dominant current" can be described without difficulty: "The Wesleyan movement is one stream in Christian history. Its point of origin is clear and its dominant current can be traced rather well. But the stream does not have neat boundaries."[2]

The "dominant current" Langford identifies is practical divinity. In so identifying the distinctive characteristic of Wesleyan theology, he performs a valuable service for all Wesleyan theologians. Today, however, the three distinctive characteristics of practical divinity are no longer central for Methodist theology. Therefore, tracing this tradition is much more difficult than Professor Langford's book suggests.

Because the Wesleyan tradition does not have clearly defined boundaries, Langford cannot provide a definitive account of "practical divinity." He does note that Wesley's *Christian Library* is the place to view Wesley's own emphasis on the importance of tradition, and there one sees that practical divinity is the distinctive characteristic.[3] Langford de-

2. Thomas A. Langford, *Practical Divinity: Theology in the Wesleyan Tradition* (Nashville: Abingdon Press, 1983), pp. 11-12.

3. Wesley, *The Christian Library* (Bristol: William Pine, 1768). The *Christian Library* was Wesley's attempt to collect central works in practical divinity and make them available for the Methodists. While this effort shows Wesley's concern for the theological education of the members of the Methodist societies, the effort was unsuccessful. Later, the *Arminian Magazine* did better what Wesley hoped the *Christian Library* would do.

scribes the *Christian Library* as the embodiment of practical divinity:

> Theology is important as it serves the interest of Christian formation. Theology is never an end, but is always a means for understanding and developing transformed living. There was little speculative interest involved in Wesley's theological investigations. He consistently turned theological reflection to practical service. Theology, in his understanding, was to be preached, sung, and lived. Consequently, volumes of the *Christian Library* are given over to actual life stories of people who embodied Christian truth.[4]

This is a suggestive description of practical divinity. For Wesley, theology was not primarily the activity of an academic elite. The emphasis of the *Christian Library* is not upon the clear and systematic articulation of doctrine. Instead, theology had a closer relationship to lived experience, which finds expression in a theology found in the form of sermons, hymns, and biographies — forms that allow theology to be understood by a great number of people. This is the function of theology as *practical* divinity; theology is produced in each generation through means that are generally accessible.

While this is an extremely suggestive account of practical divinity, the rest of Langford's book does not sufficiently assess the various currents of Wesleyan theology on the basis of the importance of practical divinity as accessible theology, found in the form of sermon, hymn, and biography. Instead, Langford views developing transformed living as the "dominant current" of practical divinity, and he assesses the various aspects of Wesleyan theology in terms of their continuity or discontinuity with this "dominant current."

But "transformed living" proves too ambiguous and indeterminate a norm against which to assess practical divinity.

---

4. Langford, *Practical Divinity*, p. 21.

19

The distinctive characteristic of Methodism becomes its ability to adjust to and transform new cultural configurations. Thus, in describing Methodism's "success" in the United States, Langford writes:

> Perhaps most important of all, Methodism was, along with the American spirit, pragmatic. Reasons for the success of the Methodist revival in North America were multiple, but among them was the fact that this movement not only adjusted to the New World but also accommodated itself to the growing edges of the new land. In these moves, Methodism separated itself from the earlier religious establishments in America.[5]

Methodism's "genius" becomes its ability to accommodate and adjust to new cultural situations because of its "practical" or "pragmatic" character. Once this understanding of practical divinity prevails, then the three characteristics of practical divinity mentioned earlier are lost. "Pragmatism" too easily replaces true practical divinity.

Of course Methodist theology "adjusted" to new cultural and social configurations; no one should deny such an obvious claim. Yet simply the capacity to "adjust" to and "accommodate" new experiences cannot provide a coherent account of a tradition. A living tradition by definition is one that is able to adjust and accommodate; if it could not, it would die. The question is *how* a tradition adjusts and accommodates. In the case of Methodism, its adjustments and accommodations too often destroyed its tradition of practical divinity.

By discussing practical divinity within the context of Wesley's *Christian Library* and American pragmatism, Langford points to a problem in Wesleyan theology. Practical divinity was at first a description of how theology was to be made accessible to as many people as possible. But soon practical divinity shifted away from this human-centered form of theo-

5. Ibid., p. 100.

logical production situated in the class meeting to a form of theology that understood its primary role to be adjustment and accommodation to the developing culture within the United States. Practical divinity became American pragmatism. Because this shift often goes unchallenged, the teaching of Methodist history, theology, and polity suffers. The central texts used to train Methodist people are constrained by the recurring attempt to portray Methodism's genius as its pragmatic ability to negotiate life in the United States. The United States' form of government becomes the norm against which Methodist polity is assessed. Thus Bishop Jack Tuell claims that United Methodist polity reflects a "representative democracy" similar to that of the United States.[6] However, Tuell's description of our polity is directly opposed to that of Francis Asbury, who supposedly implemented this representative democracy. Asbury goes to great lengths to distinguish Methodist polity — in its "nature" — from that of the nation.[7] And in contrast even to Asbury, the term *practical* has come to refer not to a theological position at all, but to an organizational style analogous to that of American culture. Bishop R. Sheldon Duecker writes: "United Methodists are practical people. They believe each component of a complicated organization needs authority to make decisions for which it is responsible."[8] Of course organizations need authority to make decisions. Who could deny such a claim? If that is all "practical" means, then it is not a very helpful notion and it should certainly not be upheld as a distinctive characteristic.

The term *practical* is used to legitimate the preoccupation

6. Jack M. Tuell, *The Organization of the United Methodist Church* (Nashville: Abingdon Press, 1985), p. 113.

7. See Francis Asbury's "Valedictory Address," in *Wesleyan Theology: A Sourcebook*, ed. Thomas A. Langford (Durham, NC: Labyrinth Press, 1984), pp. 72 and 83.

8. R. Sheldon Duecker, *Tensions in the Connection* (Nashville: Abingdon Press, 1983), p. 52.

of Methodist historians, theologians, and church leaders with church structure. Successful, pragmatic organizational skills become the defining characteristic of Wesley, who is seen primarily as an eminently practical theologian. This understanding of Wesley is used on the popular level as an excuse for inundating Methodist pastors and laity with "practical" information. But even on a scholarly level, the view of Wesley as an organizational pragmatist receives undue attention. Rupert E. Davies writes: "[John Wesley] was certainly a pragmatist, in the sense that he was always open to consider and use what was suggested to him in the form of ideas and activities. But he did not fail to put his own stamp on anything he proceeded to borrow."[9]

The amazing thing about this emphasis on Wesley's "pragmatic" spirit is not that it is a distortion, but that it is superficial.[10] For instance, Davies uses Wesley's pragmatism to defend the unsystematic nature of Wesley's themes concerning the "history, nature and design" of the "Methodist societies":

> More frequently Wesley dealt with these themes as they arose in the context of a situation in the Methodist connexion with which he had to deal, or as he sought to remove a misunderstanding in the minds of individuals, or as he rebutted criticisms that had arisen in certain quarters.[11]

But such a claim is obvious. When have theological themes not arisen "in the context of a situation," or as a response to "misunderstanding" or "criticisms"? This view of "practicality" is a weak and inoffensive characteristic in comparison to the dis-

---

9. *The Works of John Wesley,* vol. 9, ed. Rupert E. Davies (Nashville: Abingdon Press, 1989), pp. 8, 9.

10. It becomes an ideological distortion when practical divinity is primarily understood along these lines and used to secure a place within American intellectual life.

11. Davies, ed., *The Works of John Wesley,* vol. 9, p. 1.

tinctive form of theology called practical divinity. Such emphasis on Wesley's "practicality" simply serves to further the notion that the purpose of theology is to be relevant to the wider culture.

Robert C. Monk comes closer to the truth when he reminds us that practical divinity referred to "works in the thought of seventeenth- and eighteenth-century England [which] applied the truths of the Christian gospel to the daily lives of the believer or, in Wesley's words, constituted 'Christianity reduced to *practice.'* "[12] Monk is correct in pointing out a connection between Wesley's practical divinity and the seventeenth- and eighteenth-century works known as English casuistical divinity. But the word *applied* is too weak. It assumes that Christianity allows for something called "daily life" that is intelligible apart from the truth of the Christian gospel, so that the purpose of practical divinity is to "apply" this truth to that which is already present — daily life. Monk misses an important point. Practical divinity does not "apply" Christian truths to everyday life; it *constitutes* daily life. It uses the practices of parish life to construct a theology for parish life.

Monk's use of Wesley's phrase "Christianity reduced to practice" exposes the weakness of his description of practical divinity. When Wesley mentions in the *Christian Library* that he is now going to show how Christianity is "reduced to practice," he is not referring to applying the gospel to daily life; he is introducing historical accounts of Christian martyrs, men and women whose stories exemplified how much the gospel is at odds with "daily life." In light of this, how can the dominant current of Methodist theology continue to use the term *practical* to suggest that the genius of Methodism is its ability to adjust and accommodate to new situations?

12. Robert C. Monk, *John Wesley: His Puritan Heritage* (Nashville: Abingdon Press, 1966), p. 33.

## WESLEY AND PRACTICAL DIVINITY

The three characteristics of Wesley's practical divinity did not function as a capacity for adaptation to culture. Instead, they functioned as a reasonable way in which to invite the community of faith to reflect together on its journey toward holiness. As has already been mentioned, these three characteristics are as follows:

- it is a theology accessible to Methodist people in terms of style, content, and cost;

- it has a distinct purpose — holiness of heart and life, a holiness that is exemplified in the stories of faithful Christian people, and particularly the martyrs;

- the specific shape of this theology is defined by English casuistical divinity, situated within the structure of the class meeting.

Discussing Wesley's use of practical divinity along these lines should not suggest a Wesley scholasticism. I am not suggesting that Wesley's use of practical divinity must be authoritative for twentieth-century Methodism. But if tracing a tradition is theologically and historically important for Methodism, then it is also important that there be some connection between Wesley's use of practical divinity and ours. What we find is that little or no connection in fact exists; present-day Methodism evidences little *theological* tradition of practical divinity. This is disappointing because practical divinity gives us a way in which to make sense of rules such as the *Discipline*'s rejection of war and its mandate for pastors to counsel parishioners concerning military service and its alternatives.

Let me explain the various features of Wesley's use of practical divinity. First and foremost, practical divinity is theology that is generally accessible to Methodist people. Wesley wrote theology in the form of sermons and tracts so that it might be accessible to people who had neither extended academic training in theology nor resources to accumulate expensive theological literature. Still, what was contained in the sermons and tracts *was* theology.

Theology must be accessible both in an economic sense and in an intellectual sense because theology belongs to the whole church and not just to a wealthy or an academic elite. In fact, these two senses should not be separated; they are mutually reinforcing. Theology, as a true and genuine expression of the Christian faith, requires availability to Christian people.

This understanding of Wesley's use of practical divinity is readily found in *The Christian Library*. The first page of each of the fifty volumes begins with the words: "Extracts from and Abridgements of the Choicest Pieces of Practical Divinity Which Have Been Published in the English Tongue."

Wesley offers an introduction to the *Library*, and for the first few volumes he prefixes some of his own comments to the extracts. He begins his introduction with these words:

> We commonly believe, that there is not in the world, a more complete Body of Practical Divinity, than is now extant in the English Tongue, in the writings of the last and the present century. And perhaps this belief is not altogether owing to a natural prejudice in favour of our own country. It seems rather to be grounded on the truth of things, on solid, rational observation.[13]

For Wesley, "practical divinity" exists in the English tongue, but in a variety of forms. Some of it is "false," some "true," and some "truth and falsehood intermixed." Some of it only "promotes vain jangling," while true practical divinity promotes "holiness either of heart or life." Thus, there is a need for someone "to point out those only that will best reward his

13. Wesley, *The Christian Library*, vol. 1, p. i.

labours." This is what Wesley hopes to do in his *Christian Library*. He points out for those who are not well versed in theological language sound theology that will promote holiness.

Not only must people be able to purchase practical divinity, but they must also be able to understand its style and content. The content of practical divinity cannot be separated from its style. Some theology is written with such obfuscation that even if its content would promote holiness, it cannot because of the obscurity of the style. It is "scarce intelligible to the bulk of mankind." Other theologians write in a plain style but fall into another "pitfall": "their thoughts are as common as their expressions. They speak plain, but mean time they speak nothing. . . . All their observations are trite and superficial: they just skim over the surface of Religion but declare nothing of the height or depth of those great Truths which are brought to light by the Gospel." Wesley attempts to "extract the Gold out of these baser mixtures" and "separate the pure genuine Divinity out of this huge, mingled mass."

> I have endeavoured to extract such a collection of English Divinity, as (I believe) is All True, All agreeable to the Oracles of God, as is all Practical unmixt with Controversy of any kind; and all intelligible to plain men: such as is not superficial, but going down to the depth, and describing the height of Christianity; And yet not mystical, not obscure to any of those who are experienced in the ways of God.[14]

The last sentence is important. For Wesley, the *Christian Library* was not a text that could be "applied" for the production of Christian living; it was a help, a lay manual, for those who were already "experienced in the ways of God." This was a prereq-

---

14. Ibid., pp. iv-v.

uisite for understanding the function of the *Library*, a point reflected in the importance of biography throughout.

Biography serves two functions in the *Library*. The first is to highlight the importance of a person's life for his or her theology. In the majority of instances, the theological extracts begin with a short biographical sketch of the author. First the work is mentioned — for example, "Extracts from the works of Robert Bolten, B.D." — followed by the words "To which is prefixed some account of his life." The prefixed account serves to inculcate practical divinity by inseparably blending a person's lived experience with his or her articulation of the faith.

The second function of biography in the *Library* is to highlight the importance of the oppositional character of lived experience in the story of martyrs. Such stories constitute the bulk of the first six volumes. These stories promote the virtues of "courage and constancy" necessary for Christian living. In his introduction to works of Clement, Polycarp, and Ignatius, Wesley includes accounts of the martyrdom of the latter two, explaining that his purpose is to add "their courage and constancy" to "the maintaining of the general piety of their lives and care for the purity of religion." Wesley hoped that these stories would capture people and compel them toward a vision of God.

After his discussion of the martyrdom of Ignatius and Polycarp, Wesley includes the homilies of Macarius and John Arndt's "True Christianity." Then for the next four volumes he includes nothing but stories of martyrdom. He explains his purpose thus:

> After the venerable Remains of Ignatius and Polycarp closed with the artless, yet lively Discourses of Macarius, and John Arndt's nervous account of True Christianity, worthy of the Earliest Ages; I believed nothing could be more acceptable to the serious reader than to see this Christianity reduced to *Practice*. I was therefore easily determined to subjoin to these,

The Acts and Monuments of the Christian Martyrs. Here we see that pure and amiable Religion, evidently set forth before our Eyes; Assaulted indeed by all the powers of Earth and Hell, but more than Conquerors over all. May we all learn from these Worthies, To be not almost only, but altogether Christians! To reckon all Things but Dung and Dross for the Excellency of the *Experimental* Knowledge of Jesus Christ. And not to count our Lives dear unto our Selves, so we may finish our course with joy.[15]

This is a powerful description of practical divinity, and it exposes the inadequacy of Monk's definition of practical theology as theology applied to daily life. Wesley understood practical divinity not as application, adjustment, or accommodation but as a lived, experimental knowledge of Christ resulting in confrontation with the "powers of Earth and Hell." The martyrs' lives are the context for practical divinity, and their stories are to inculcate the same sense of "courage, constancy, and joy" in other believers, heightening the tension between the Christian life and the "powers of Earth and Hell."

This tension is brought to the fore in the story of John Foxe contained in the *Christian Library*. Here the author invites readers to pay particular attention to "two special points": "First to observe the Disposition and Nature of this World; Secondly the Nature and Condition of the Kingdom of Christ: The Vanity of the one, and the establishment of the other; the unquiet State of the one ruled by Man's Violence and Wisdom, and the happy success of the other, ever ruled by God's Blessing and Providence."[16] Practical divinity does not help one adjust to culture; rather, it helps one understand the tension that arises between the journey toward holiness and the visions of other journeys that capture our imagination.

The preceding discussion of practical divinity in the *Chris-*

15. Ibid., vol. 2, p. 216.
16. Ibid.

*tian Library* also presupposes and further clarifies Wesley's theology in his sermons. The statement "be not almost only, but altogether Christian" refers to his second sermon in the *Sermons on Several Occasions,* "The Almost Christian." This sermon, like much of Wesley's work, is filled with pious generalities, such as the claim that "love of God," "love of neighbor," and "faith" are necessary to be "altogether Christian" rather than "almost Christian." In fact, the sermon by itself is basically useless because of the level of superficiality within it. However, against the backdrop of the stories of martyrdom in the *Christian Library,* these pious generalities become more concrete. Certain phrases take on a new significance:

> Now whosoever has this faith which "purifies the heart", by the power of God who dwelleth therein, from pride, anger, desire, "from all unrighteousness", "from all filthiness of flesh and spirit"; which fills it with love stronger than death both to God and to all mankind — love that doth the works of God, glorying to spend and to be spent for all men, and that endureth with joy, not only the reproach of Christ, the being mocked, despised, and hated of all men, but whatsoever the wisdom of God permits the malice of men or devils to inflict; whosoever has this faith, thus "working by love", is not *almost* only, but *altogether* a Christian.[17]

Once the stories of the martyrs are understood as the context for this passage, Wesley's description of Christian love moves from mere pious generality to an alternative way of life that conflicts with those powers of earth and hell that are marked by violence. Love of God and neighbor produces the fruit of "reproach" when that which despises God despises the person following God. How then could "practical divinity" be pri-

17. "The Almost Christian," in *The Works of John Wesley,* vol. 1, ed. Albert C. Outler (Nashville: Abingdon Press, 1984), p. 139.

marily concerned with cultural accommodation and adjustment?

In addition to general accessibility in style and content — embodied in the importance of biography — practical divinity is also characterized by a specific understanding of theology known as English casuistical divinity, found among the Caroline divines of the sixteenth and seventeenth centuries. "Practical divinity" is no new term coined by Wesley; it was common parlance for seventeenth-century casuistical divinity. In *The Structure of Caroline Moral Theology*, H. R. McAdoo writes: "What strikes the moral theologian with fresh force the further he penetrates, is the universal interest of the seventeenth century in 'practical divinity' and the importance accorded to it officially and parochially throughout the period."[18] When Susanna Wesley wrote to John urging him to study "Practical Divinity," the study of this specific theology is what she meant. Wesley did study this theology, particularly the work of Jeremy Taylor, and he wrote in his journal that Taylor was the impetus behind the first Oxford group.

English casuistical divinity had two characteristics. First, it was primarily parish centered. It worked from the resources of parish life and it primarily addressed parish life. It presupposed Christians banding together in small groups to discuss cases of conscience in an attempt to examine everyday life through the sermon heard on Sunday. As another casuist, Richard Baxter, wrote in his journal: "Every Thursday evening my Neighbours that were most desirous and had opportunity, met at my House, and there one of them repeated the Sermon; and afterwards they proposed what Doubts any of them had about the Sermon, or any other Case of Conscience and I resolved their Doubts." Casuistry was not a systematic, academic discipline. It was an oral practice rooted in the flow of parish

18. H. R. McAdoo, *The Structure of Caroline Moral Theology* (London: Longmans, Green, 1949), p. xi.

life, and it required the bodily presence of people to discuss and debate how they were to practice the divinity they learned through participation in parish life.

The second characteristic of English casuistical divinity is its "legalistic" nature. This type of theology can be found in such works as William Perkins's *A Discourse of Conscience and The Whole Treatise of Cases of Conscience,* as well as Jeremy Taylor's *Ductor Dubitantium.* The structure of such works takes the form of principles that are to assist Christians in negotiating cases of conscience. These works answer questions that often begin with the phrase "Whether it be lawful to. . . ." Thus English casuistical divinity is similar in structure to the book of Leviticus, the early penitentials, and Jesuit casuistry.[19]

Wesley includes this form of theology in the *Christian Library.* Volume eight contains a work by the English casuist Robert Bolton entitled "Instruction for comforting Afflicted Consciences." Volume nine includes another of Bolton's works — "A Treatise on Self-Examination." Volume eleven includes a casuistical work of Theodore Goodwin entitled, "The Causes by which, The Cases wherein, and the ends for which, God leaves his children to Distresses of Conscience."

While the structure of English casuistical divinity is "legalistic," it is legalistic in a pejorative sense only when it is divorced from its social context — the class meeting — and its purpose — holiness of heart and life. The social context of parish life and the purpose of holiness prevent casuistry from

---

19. Interestingly, when Wesley explained why his Oxford group was called "Methodist" he referred to a sect of Roman physicians known as "Methodists" who developed the principle "contraries cure contraries." This principle was central to the development of the early penitentials. See John T. McNeill and Helena M. Gamer, eds., *Medieval Handbooks of Penance* (New York: Columbia University Press, 1938), p. 44. See also Wesley's "On Laying the Foundation of the New Chapel," in *The Works of John Wesley,* vol. 3, ed. Albert C. Outler (Nashville: Abingdon Press, 1986), pp. 579-92. This will be discussed further in Chapter 4.

becoming a rigid legalism, because casuistical divinity establishes principles or "rules" in order to engage people in an argument about how to practice Christianity daily. This is why Wesley included biography and an accessible style in the *Christian Library* as well as casuistical works. The biographies keep casuistry from legalism by keeping a view of the purpose of casuistry before the reader. The stories of the martyrs, as well as devotional literature such as Jeremy Taylor's *Rules for Holy Living and Dying*, formulated the end that the principles served. Abstracted from the end of holiness, the principles make no sense. This is important to keep in mind because moral philosophy developed out of practical divinity — but it abstracted the principles from the specific end of holiness.

Albert Jonsen and Stephen Toulmin narrate the story of this shift by noting that in 1839 when "William Whewell was elected to the Knightbridge Chair of Casuistic Divinity, he found it necessary to change his title to Professor of Moral Philosophy." The reason for this shift, they suggest, was due to the general shift "away from resolving particular questions of moral choice to the construction of general theories of morality."[20] Wesley was not concerned with general theories of morality. He was interested in practical divinity, which sought to resolve cases of conscience through the cultivation of "holy tempers" for the purpose of holiness of heart and life, with a vision of that life defined by the story of the martyrs in the *Christian Library*.

Practical divinity as casuistry is more than merely the articulation of principles. It requires a specific social context amenable to its nature as a confessional exercise. For Methodist theology, this social context is the class meeting. The class meeting includes discussion of the "rules" that bind people together in a common journey, but the "rules" only establish the general shape of the discussion. The people in the class meeting who

20. Albert T. Jonsen and Stephen Toulmin, *The Abuse of Casuistry* (Berkeley: University of California Press, 1988), p. 163.

interpret and live the rules are an essential element of casuistical divinity. Historians such as H. R. McAdoo who suggest that practical divinity died out at the end of the seventeenth century are certainly correct, but only to the extent that the popular theology articulated in the Methodist Rules of the United Societies and embodied in the class meeting is neglected.[21]

The practice of casuistry is found in the early Methodist class meeting. What are the "principles" and "practices" of a Methodist? asked Wesley. "He is inwardly and outwardly conformed to the will of God, as revealed in the written Word. He *thinks, speaks, and lives according to the* 'method' *laid down in the revelation of Jesus Christ."*[22] Of course, this "method" is more specific than Wesley here asserts in "The Character of a Methodist." The "method" is better seen in the Rules of the Societies. These rules begin with the claim: "The design of our meeting is to obey that command of God, 'Confess your faults one to another, and pray one for another that ye may be healed.' "[23] And the rules themselves are penitential disciplines, as rule 4 shows clearly: "To speak, each of us in order, freely and plainly the true state of our soul, with the faults we have committed in thought, word, or deed, and the temptations we have felt since our last meeting." Such a discussion is casuistry.

Practical divinity provides a way of making sense of the rejection of war in Article 16 of the United Methodist Confession of Faith. This article is not to be rigorously applied to each Methodist to determine her or his membership; rather, it is a rule providing guidance and purpose for our communal life. The rule assesses our own faithfulness and opens up new possibilities for Christian living. We may not all live the rule at present, but the rule's presence is a constant reminder that this is the life we are to embody. We do not seek to make the rule

21. The fact that we still have General Rules in our *Discipline* shows that a residual element of practical divinity still remains in our tradition.
22. Davies, ed., *The Works of John Wesley,* vol. 9, p. 41.
23. Ibid., p. 77.

relevant to us; instead, we penitentially seek to make our lives relevant to the rule — to this measure of faithful discipleship handed down to us. The rule only points to ways in which we still need to cultivate "holy tempers" and invites us to do penance for the lack of such tempers as we wait on God's grace to lay a seed in us that will issue in peaceableness.

Practical divinity is a parish-centered theology, accessible to all Christian pilgrims, that debates and discusses the most appropriate way to practice Christianity among the community of faith. Why have we lost this understanding of theology? A myriad of responses could be given, but one important response is that United Methodism abandoned practical divinity through its efforts to be relevant to the wider culture, and especially to the dominant philosophy within American life — pragmatism.[24] Pragmatism seeks to adjust and accommodate philosophy to everyday life. It does not have the purpose of "holiness of heart or life"; it only seeks to be "effective."[25]

24. I realize that there are many varieties of "pragmatism" and thus this statement needs to be nuanced. C. S. Pierce, William James, John Dewey, Richard Rorty, Barbara Hernstein Smith, and Cornell West are all pragmatists and their philosophical positions are different and quite sophisticated. I find West's pragmatism particularly compelling. Rather than launch into a discussion of the various forms of pragmatism, I will simply assert that the problem with the replacement of practical divinity by pragmatism is that the purpose for the Christian life is lost to a philosophy that seeks to begin with the everyday activity of life and go from there. Practical divinity and some forms of pragmatism are very similar, but the differences are such that the replacement of the former by the latter drastically shifts Methodist theology.

25. Perhaps the most influential and important pragmatist in United Methodism today is Lyle Schaller. His work is a prime example of the transition from practical divinity to pragmatism. Even though he offers many interesting insights into the contemporary situation, his work "is based on the assumption that the individual who holds a reasonably accurate view of the nature of contemporary reality will be able to design the appropriate course of action" (Schaller, *It's a Different World* [Nashville: Abingdon Press, 1987], p. 19). Schaller assumes that "contemporary reality" can be known through statistics and surveys, and thus he plunges our church further into a supply-side ecclesiology by first defining the needs of the culture and then applying Christianity at a secondary level to those needs.

Pragmatism does not need "rules," nor does it need the story of the martyrs to remind people of the purpose of the rules.

Pragmatism has some real advantages as a philosophy. It can be accessible to a large number of people because it seeks to begin with everyday life and adjust philosophy accordingly, rather than beginning with a supreme principle from which others are deduced in a logical fashion. But pragmatism is not a theology. Theology requires the purpose of holiness of heart and life. And holiness requires the story of God's dealings with Israel and with us in Jesus. These stories are not to be adjusted to be relevant to everyday life; they are to constitute our everyday life. We are to be adjusted to fit these stories and not vice versa. That is a painful practice; constant adjustments are needed to make us fit such stories, and penance allows us to make these adjustments. The mandate to counsel parishioners concerning military service, as well as the article that reminds us that war and bloodshed are contrary to the spirit and gospel of Christ, are reminders to us of the story we have inherited.

In this chapter we have explored the nature of practical divinity and narrated how it was lost through a shift to pragmatism and practicality. But there is an additional reason for our loss of practical divinity. In the nineteenth century, the purpose of our discipline shifted from participation in holiness to participation in civilization. Once the purpose shifted, practical divinity became a theology no longer accessible to the Methodist people; rather, we sought audience with the cultural and political elite. The audience for our *Discipline* became senators and presidents. Thus the structure that rendered our theology intelligible was not the class meeting as a penitential practice but the United States government with its emphasis on freedom of individual conscience. Before we can suggest ways in which a theology of discipline can be reclaimed, we must narrate the story of the loss of holiness and the "gain" of civilization. To this story we now turn in Chapter 2.

CHAPTER TWO

# To Discipline or to Civilize?

In 1816, when the Evangelical Association was formed, its members created a Confession of Faith patterned after the Methodist Articles of Religion. In 1839, they added a statement to Article 16 of their Confession that read, "We believe that wars and bloodshed are not agreeable to the Gospel and Spirit of Christ."[1] The revised article remained throughout most of the history of the Evangelical Association; however, it was replaced for a brief time during the Civil War by an article that read, "it is the imperative duty of our Government, to use the sword entrusted to it of God, . . . and it is the holiest duty of every citizen, faithfully to support the Government in the important duties devolving upon the same."[2] This change allowed members of the church to participate in warfare without violating the Confession of Faith. After the war the 1839 edition of Article 16 returned, and it survived through both the 1946 merger with the United Brethren Church to form the Evangelical United Brethren Church and the 1968 merger of that church with the Methodists to form the United Methodist Church.

At the time of the 1968 merger, the Methodists did not have any constitutional statements on war. During the early part of the

1. J. Bruce Behney and Paul H. Eller, *The History of the Evangelical United Brethren Church* (Nashville: Abingdon Press, 1979), p. 147.
2. Ibid., p. 199.

twentieth century they did make "official" statements.[3] These early statements are a mixed blessing. On the one hand, they reveal the extraordinary courage of the early twentieth-century Methodists: the statements reject war as incompatible with the Christian gospel.[4] On the other hand, the theology that grounds this courageous stand is questionable. This questionable theological foundation is one reason why the Methodists adjusted their *Discipline* during World War II from the courageous stance against war to asserting the necessity to take up arms.

## THE DEVELOPMENT OF METHODIST STATEMENTS ON WAR

In its Thirty-nine Articles, the Church of England has a clear and normative position on war set forth in Article 37, "Of the Power of the Civil Magistrates":

> The King's Majesty hath the chief power in this Realm of England and, other his Dominions, unto whom the chief Government of all Estates of this Realm, whether they be Ecclesiastical or Civil, in all causes doth appertain, and is not, nor ought to be, subject to any foreign Jurisdiction. Where we attribute to the King's majesty the chief government, by which Title we understand the minds of some slanderous folks to be offended; we give not our Princes the ministering either of God's Word, or of the Sacraments, the which thing the Injunctions also lately set forth by Elizabeth our Queen do most plainly testify; but that only prerogative which we see to have been given always to all

3. Unlike Article 16, these early statements are not legally binding; they only bear the weight of tradition.

4. The current disciplinary statements found in the Social Principles and in par. 439.i are direct descendants of these earlier statements. They have been abridged over the years to take their current form.

godly Princes in holy Scriptures by God himself; that is, that they should rule all estates and degrees committed to their charge by God whether they be Ecclesiastical or Temporal, and restrain with the civil sword the stubborn and evil-doers.

The Bishop of Rome hath no jurisdiction in this Realm of England.

The Laws of the Realm may punish Christian men with death, for heinous and grievous offences.

*It is lawful for Christian men, at the commandment of the Magistrate, to wear weapons, and serve in the wars.*[5]

When Wesley sent his twenty-four Articles of Religion, abridged from the Anglican thirty-nine, to the newly formed Methodist Episcopal Church, he omitted Article 37 for obvious reasons — loyalty to the king was not a popular notion in America in 1784.[6] Thus at its inception the Methodist Episcopal Church was not burdened with an official just war position in service of the magistrate.

The Methodists did soon add an article called "Of the Rulers of the United States of America" to the twenty-four Wesley established. It states:

The President, the Congress, the general assemblies, the governors, and the councils of state, *as the delegates of the people,* are the rulers of the United States of America, according to the division of power made to them by the Constitu-

5. *The Book of Common Prayer;* emphasis added. Notice that this supposed "just war" article mentions nothing about just war; it only states that the magistrate can command Christians to go to war.
6. For an account of the twenty-four articles Wesley sent over, see "John Wesley's Sunday Service of the Methodists in North America," *Quarterly Review* (1984).

tion of the United States and by the constitutions of their respective states. And the said states are a sovereign and independent nation, and ought not to be subject to any foreign jurisdiction.[7]

Interestingly, this new article stipulates that Methodism respects the rule of the United States, but it omits the Anglican law that required the bearing of arms at the request of the magistrate. Certainly this is more than a mere oversight, for the people who drafted this constitution were aware of the Anglican stance. The lack of anything similar to the Anglican Article 37 suggests that the early Methodists did not believe that the government had the right to require Christians to bear arms.

The Methodist Article 23 was the only constitutional stance establishing the relationship between the state and the church. It was silent on the question of war. In the Uniting Conference of 1939 — which brought together the Methodist Protestant Church, the Methodist Episcopal Church, and the Methodist Episcopal Church South — Article 23 was amended, interpreting it "to our churches in foreign lands." The amendment, which is a legislative enactment and not part of our constitution, reads:

> It is the duty of all Christians, and especially of all Christian ministers, to observe and obey the laws and commands of the governing or supreme authority of the country of which they are citizens or subjects or in which they reside, and to use all laudable means to encourage and enjoin obedience to the powers that be.[8]

Once again the Methodists were silent on the question of war. All that this amendment says is that "all laudable means" are to be used to enjoin obedience; it says nothing about the use of

---

7. Article 23 of the Articles of Religion, in the *Book of Discipline*.
8. *Book of Discipline*, p. 68.

force. The term "laudable means" is ambiguous, but it certainly does not suggest that Christians are required to fight in war.

In 1968, when the Evangelical United Brethren (EUB) and the Methodists merged to become the United Methodists, the silence concerning participation in war was broken. The EUB Confession of Faith was adopted as an established doctrinal standard protected by the constitution. Thus Article 16 of the United Methodist Confession of Faith provides a constitutional theological understanding of the relationship between church and state that proscribes Christian participation in war. The article acknowledges that government is ordained of God — "We believe civil government derives its just powers from the Sovereign God" — but it adds the stipulation that the "just powers" from which government derives are "based on, and responsible for, the recognition of human rights under God." In light of this basis for ordained government, the article then rejects theology such as is found in the Church of England, where the magistrate may legally require Christians "to wear weapons and serve in the wars," and instead claims, "We believe war and bloodshed are contrary to the gospel and spirit of Christ." What then can the magistrate expect of Christians? "It is the duty of Christian citizens to give *moral* strength and purpose to their respective governments through *sober, righteous* and *godly living.*"

This has been United Methodism's official stance on war since the 1968 merger with the Evangelical United Brethren Church. The EUB had a relationship with the historic peace churches, and that relationship is reflected in Article 16. This should lead us to consider seriously if we are not, in fact, by historical contingency and by the leading of the Holy Spirit, now fully within the realm of the historic peace churches.

While an argument could be made that since 1968 the United Methodist Church has been constitutionally a pacifist church, the story of "official" Methodist statements on war in the twentieth century both support and deny such a claim. Not until the early part of the twentieth century did the church actually develop a statement directly addressing the question of war and peace. Because of Methodism's upward mobility during the latter part of the nineteenth century, its incredible increase in wealth, and its phenomenal growth, the need arose to address the question of whether this large and influential church permitted or prohibited participation in war. Many of the senators and representatives of the United States government on both the state and federal level were Methodists.[9] The church found it imperative to offer them guidance on the perplexing questions of war and peace. From all accounts, these Methodists actually took what the church had to say seriously. This says something positive about the ability of the church to cultivate its people into the discipline of peace at the beginning of this century. Unfortunately, the main theological theme present in the church's *Discipline* was not the purpose of holiness of heart and life, but the imperative to preserve "civilization."

"Civilization" rather than holiness became the dominant theological category. The place of discipline as a means of grace binding people together on a common journey from sin to holiness was replaced by the notion of the progress of civilization into liberal democracy, and the necessity to sustain this progress. This leads to an ironic twist in the history of Methodism — the church's success in disciplining its members into the dominant theological notion of civilization is precisely what destroyed the ability of the church to discipline its members at all; for central to the notion of civilization is the freedom of the individual from all external forms of discipline. Now as we find ourselves in a post-Christian civilization, we realize that a theological account of discipline is necessary to regain our identity, but our success in disciplining people into liberal democratic thought prevents us from regaining that identity.

9. For a highly laudatory description of this, see the 1908 Episcopal Address in the General Conference Minutes of the Methodist Episcopal Church (Nashville: Abingdon Press, 1908).

The development of Methodist statements on war in the *Discipline* reveals how this situation came about.

## CIVILIZATION AND ITS CONTENTS

A doctrine of "civilization" underlies the Methodist statements on war. These statements contain two themes: (1) unequivocal condemnations of war, and (2) unequivocal affirmations of the inviolability of individual conscience. These two themes support the doctrine of civilization. For early twentieth-century liberal theology, civilization means the freedom of the individual from all constraints so that the consent of his or her will is the sole authority of government. Because civilization means the inviolable sanctity of individual freedom from all external authority, unequivocal statements can be made with incredible alacrity, since they have only "persuasive" authority.

In Methodism, one of the first references to military intervention is found in the 1908 Episcopal Address of the Methodist Episcopal Church. The bishops lauded Theodore Roosevelt for his "successful efforts to bring the Russo-Japanese War to an end." And they expressed complete approval of Andrew Carnegie's construction of a site "for the peace tribunals which are to meet at The Hague." Central to their support of peace and their admiration of Carnegie and Roosevelt is the doctrine of civilization:

> Distant as the day seems when "they shall beat their swords into plowshares, and their spears into pruning hooks: nation shall not lift up a sword against nations, neither shall they learn war any more," it is yet evident by the creation of the Hague Tribunal and by the revisions of the laws of war, that the conscience of the nations are more sensitive as to the wickedness of war than at any other time; that strong efforts are being made to diminish its evils, both on sea and on land, and that the spread of democratic ideas is such that very soon rulers will not be able to go to war without the consent

of those whose bodies must pay the cost in labor, wounds and death.[10]

The bishops' address suggests that Isaiah's vision is yet to be fulfilled, and that it will be fulfilled through *the spread of democratic ideas*. The bishops' vision of peace is not grounded primarily on Christological arguments; instead it is supported by the implementation of a public policy, the spreading of civilization — that is, democratic ideas. Peace is the goal of the progress of civilization, and democracy as found in the United States is central to that progress.

Rather than utilizing the art of Christian theology, the bishops' argument is more akin to Western political philosophy such as that found in Immanuel Kant's *Eternal Peace*. Kant thought that with the appropriate republican constitution, in which individual conscience was held as the authoritative principle in government, peace would naturally follow:

the republican constitution does offer the prospect of the desired purpose, that is to say, eternal peace, and the reason is as follows: If, as is necessarily the case under the constitution, the consent of the citizens is required in order to decide whether there should be war or not, nothing is more natural than that those who would have to decide to undergo all the deprivations of war will very much hesitate to start such an evil game. For the deprivations are many, such as fighting oneself, paying for the cost of the war out of one's own possessions, and repairing the devastations which it costs, and to top all the evils there remains a burden of debts which embitters the peace and can never be paid off on account of approaching new wars. By contrast, under a constitution where the subject is not a citizen and which is therefore not republican, it is the easiest thing in the world to start a war.[11]

10. General Conference Minutes of the Methodist Episcopal Church, 1908, pp. 134-35.
11. Immanuel Kant, *Eternal Peace*, in *The Philosophy of Kant*, ed. Carl J. Friedrich (New York: Modern Library, 1949), p. 438.

The bishops' claim that "very soon rulers will not be able to go to war without the consent of those whose bodies must pay the cost in labor, wounds and death" comes very close to Kant's view of political government. I seriously doubt that the bishops read *Eternal Peace* in preparation for their address. The similarity between their statement and Kantian philosophy reflects the pervasive assumption during the nineteenth and early twentieth centuries that with the appropriate public policy, ignorance and violence would be overcome and peace would be possible.

Perhaps we should not judge our forebears too harshly for this position, which most political theorists and theologians now judge as utopian. Has the "realist" political view contributed to the preservation of peace in any more substantial way than the Kantian view? It has not. Nor has it contributed any less to the warring between nations. At least the Kantian theory creates an expectation of peace. The "realist" view too quickly acquiesces to the inevitability of war. Yet the "realist" view was made possible in part because of the ineffectual outcome of the Kantian theory. World War II empirically proved Kant's theory wrong. War is not a result of inadequate political constitutions but of something deeper within human existence — Christian theology calls it "sin." Insofar as theologians who accepted the Kantian theory neglected the necessary theological category of sin, they subordinated Christianity to a secular political philosophy.

The bishops' affirmation of the development of an international forum was admirable. However, their view of the sensitivity of nations' consciences is utopian given the nature of international relations over the next three decades. Their address did not lead to any official church stance on the participation of its members in war. Yet when the official stance was developed in 1924, the Kantian theory was once again the guiding principle. The 1924 statement begins with this claim:

> Millions of our fellow men have died heroically in "a war to end war." What they undertook must be finished by methods

of peace. War is not inevitable. It is the supreme enemy of mankind. Its futility is beyond question. Its continuance is the suicide of civilization. We are determined to outlaw the whole war system.[12]

In this statement, war is wrong because it threatens the continuance of civilization; the statement fails to understand war as an expression of our sinful desire to secure our own life rather than accept God's peaceable presence in Christ. Instead of denouncing war in theological terms, the 1924 statement denounces war as strategically ineffective for the onward progress of civilization.[13] The statement says this clearly in its concluding paragraph: war challenges the "principles of brotherhood," and this means that "The progress of the kingdom of Jesus Christ is clearly at stake."

Because peace is understood as a goal to be accomplished through an effective political strategy, the response of the church is linked to the nation. This is made clear in the 1924 statement: "The *nation and the Church* can do now what they may never, never be able to do again."[14] The 1924 petition is addressed to the president of the United States, the U.S. Senate, and the Permanent Court of International Justice. Thus politicians, rather than the people called Methodist, represent the primary audience for this statement. Here we come across a fundamental principle of the doctrine of civilization. Rather than addressing the question of war in the context of the cultivation of holiness among the members of the church, the 1924 statement — and those that follow it — assume that their pri-

---

12. *Book of Discipline of the Methodist Episcopal Church* (Nashville: The Methodist Publishing House, 1924), p. 589.

13. John Howard Yoder offers a decisive critique of this form of pacifism in his chapter called "Liberal Protestant Pacifism" in *Christian Attitudes to War, Peace, and Revolution: A Companion to Bainton* (Elkhart, IN: Co-op Bookstore, 1983).

14. 1924 *Book of Discipline*, p. 590; emphasis added.

mary task is to speak to political leaders. Therefore, unlike practical divinity, which is to be available to all believers, the doctrine of civilization seeks audience with the cultural and political elite.

When we find statements in the United Methodist *Discipline* such as "war is incompatible with the example and teaching of Christ," we rightly suspect that the audience for such statements is not the Methodist people but lawmakers and policymakers. When we read that war is incompatible with the gospel but that Methodists are free to participate in war as long as they do so "conscientiously," our suspicions are confirmed.[15] Such statements appear as residual elements of a church that now resembles, as Paul Ramsey once said, the left wing of the Democratic party at prayer. Many of us are afraid that endorsing paragraph 439.i — "To counsel concerning military service and its alternatives" — is to endorse that vision imposed from on high, and that vision is not one we want to endorse. We were not baptized into the Democratic party.

If the purpose of the disciplinary statement on war is to construct public policy rather than to bind individual Methodists together on a common journey from sin to holiness, then the *Discipline* has lost its theological integrity and become just one more handbook for public policymakers. The fact that the 1924 petition was addressed to politicians makes clear that, from their origin, the Methodist statements on war were meant for policymakers and not for church people. The only reference to the church in this statement is the suggestion that a "prayer for peace be prepared and used at every communion service." This request for a prayer for peace at communion was controversial. An amendment came before the General Conference proposing that it be stricken because the special commission was only requested to speak on the problem of war and not to address the church directly. One cannot help but surmise that

15. See the *Book of Discipline*, par. 70.g.

any general statement on war would not be as controversial as this desire for prayer, because that would actually affect the Methodist people. In fact, at the same time that the General Conference passed the 1924 statement on war it also passed a petition at the request of the military to increase the number of chaplains in the military for the purpose of "augmenting and strengthening of the forces."[16] Thus the statement against war was obviously not intended to have any impact on the actual practice of the Methodist ministry, let alone on the lives of Methodist members. If we can only keep our statements at a sufficiently abstract level, then we can be as unequivocal in our denunciation of war as we want because everyone knows our position will never be embodied in the people called Methodist.

One amendment to the official 1924 statement was suggested:

> And true to the insistent advocacy of our Church for law and orderliness in the State and nation, and its loyalty to the Constitution of our Republic in the past, we declare that one of the effective means which have aided in the development of civilization out of the chaos, injustice, and wrongs of the past has been through law and its enforcement, and we make urgent call upon all people of our nation to consecrate their efforts toward the maintenance of the laws of the land.[17]

The proposed amendment was tabled; but its author, J. D. Black, was correct in pointing out that this "civilization" the church was so concerned to protect through the banishment of war had itself been achieved to a large extent through violent means. He rightly noted that if the statement on war was concerned with "the development of civilization," then the church should recognize that force and violence were part of that development. The creation of "civilization" employed "effective

16. Journal of the General Conference, 1924, pp. 234-35.
17. Ibid., p. 375.

means" through the use of force, violence, and coercion against those branded "uncivilized." To use the doctrine of civilization without accepting this is to have a very selective memory.

## PERSONALISM AND THE DOCTRINE OF CIVILIZATION

Although the Methodist bishops who prepared the 1908 Episcopal Address did not develop the doctrine of civilization by reading Kant and directly appropriating his work, an influential form of Methodist theology known as Boston personalism did directly incorporate Kant's work. A. C. Knudsen, for example, wrote a book entitled *The Philosophy of War and Peace* that, in substance, was similar to Kant's *Eternal Peace*. While the pervasive assumption of Kantian political theory offered a dominant way in which the majority of people thought about issues of war and peace, the theology of Boston personalism augmented that assumption. Thus, as we continue to narrate the story of "civilization" in Methodist statements on war, the theological contribution of the personalists must be noted. I am not claiming that Boston personalism created the doctrine of civilization; I am arguing that Boston personalism represented a doctrine present in American culture and gave it articulate expression.

One of the most influential theological proponents of the doctrine of civilization was Borden Parker Bowne, who began the school of personalism. He was a Methodist layperson who studied in Germany in the latter part of the nineteenth century and returned to the United States to develop a theology that held great power in Methodist schools and seminaries through much of the twentieth century. Both he and his student, A. C. Knudsen, found the essence of the Christian message in moral progress.

In *The Atonement*, Bowne follows Adolph von Harnack in

seeking to distinguish the "abiding truth" of the Atonement from the "changing form of its expression." This "changing form" — found in "popular religious speech" and "popular hymns" — Bowne rejects. In its place he points to some essence beneath theological language that he calls "the moral meaning."[18] Bowne describes this "moral meaning" in his book *The Immanence of God:* "a divine purpose, a moral development in humanity is the essential meaning of God in history."[19] Thus he essentializes Christianity into the transition from an uncivilized to a civilized culture.

Bowne offers the doctrine of civilization as the essence of Christianity. But Bowne was more honest than the 1924 General Conference committee who tabled Black's amendment, for he understood that war held an important place within the doctrine of civilization. In 1892 he wrote:

> In the development of humanity wars have often been necessary. Wars of self-defence have been waged by the civilized nations against the barbarous hordes, and it is only a short time since the barbarous and uncivilized races were so definitely put under foot as to be no longer a source of danger. Modern science in its military applications has finally rescued civilization from danger at the hands of outside barbarians. Other wars have arisen in the way of securing the rights of humanity and the industrial development demanded by civilization. Both of these types of war have been historically necessary and beneficent, and both are morally justifiable. The professional philanthropist in his denunciation of war sometimes overlooks this fact, and unites all wars in the one class of butchery and murder. This folly and falsehood prevent the truth he has from being recognized. War for passion's sake is only animal ferocity. War for ambition's sake is the

18. Borden Parker Bowne, *The Atonement* (New York: Eaton and Mains, 1900), p. 3.
19. Borden Parker Bowne, *The Immanence of God* (Boston: Houghton Mifflin, 1905), p. 52.

sum of all crimes. But there are other wars than these, and wars which have been among the most beneficent events of human history. With the progress of humanity we may hope that the last type of war will no longer be necessary, and that the former types will be made impossible.[20]

Bowne realized that any account of the doctrine of civilization had to appreciate the way in which war made civilization possible. The genocide of Native Americans and the enslavement of African Americans were not simply incidental to the accumulation of capital and the development of liberal democracy that gave rise to the United States as a world power. Bowne was honest; we could now have peace because we had destroyed our enemies — the "uncivilized barbarians." Yet Bowne was convinced that the barbarians had, in fact, been defeated. This meant that peace might be possible if the "progress of humanity" continued.

Hand in hand with the theology of Boston personalism was that of Walter Rauschenbusch. Methodism drank deeply from this well. Rauschenbusch, a Baptist, was suspicious of Methodism, for he believed the American churches were part and parcel of the American nation.[21] Methodism had bishops and this was distinctly un-American. Yet Rauschenbusch acknowledged that it was the Methodists through their 1908 adoption of "The Social Creed" who most embodied his view of "social Christianity." "The honor of making the first ringing declaration" of the rise of social Christianity, Rauschenbusch

20. Borden Parker Bowne, *The Principles of Ethics* (New York: Harper and Brothers, 1896), p. 300.

21. In *Christianizing the Social Order* (New York: Macmillan, 1912), Rauschenbusch wrote: "The American churches are part of the American nation. They are not a foreign clerical organization grafted on our national life, but an essential part of it from the beginning, a great plastic force which has molded our public opinions and our institutions from the foundation up" (p. 7).

wrote, "belongs to the Methodist Church North."[22] The spirit of the Social Creed, as well as the development of the statements on war, partakes of Rauschenbusch's social understanding of Christianity.

This social understanding also had as its fundamental premise the doctrine of the progress of civilization. Rauschenbusch wrote: "We are apt to think that progress is the natural thing. Progress is more than natural. It is divine." The purpose of social Christianity is not to stand in the way of the natural progress of civilization.

> The most important and persistent obstacle of progress is the conservative stupidity and stolidity of human nature. In history, as in physics, the *vis inertiae* rules. . . . There are nations and races that have not changed appreciably for ages.[23]

Theologians such as Rauschenbusch and Bowne provided the discursive structure upon which Methodist pacifism was based during the early part of the twentieth century. If their doctrine of civilization, grounded in the superiority of American culture, were only incidental to their work it could be overlooked, for they were both men who were responsible for tremendous social achievements in the lives of working-class people. But the idea of the progress of "our Western civilization" was central to their theology.

The progressivist view provided the base for pacifism because "our civilization" was supposedly so successful and so fixed that war would no longer be necessary for its continuance. All right-thinking people would agree that "our civilization" was the best. Thus as long as right-thinking people remained in power, civilization was secure. In fact, in an extremely disturbing paragraph, Bowne rules out political rights for all people of "low grade intelligence":

22. Ibid., pp. 13-14.
23. Ibid., p. 30.

A low grade of intelligence, also, justly excludes from political rights. Such persons are only disturbing factors in society, and when numerous they constitute a grave social menace. Their ignorance leaves them an easy prey to passion, and hence an easy prey to demagogue.[24]

And in a letter that makes us all uneasy, Rauschenbusch identified the superiority of Western civilization with the superiority of "whites":

> Is the American stock so fertile that it will people this continent alone? . . . Are the whites of this continent so sure of their possession against the blacks of the South and the seething yellow flocks beyond the Pacific that they need no reenforcement of men of their own blood while yet it is time?[25]

Clearly the doctrine of civilization that was central to the work of Bowne and Rauschenbusch had an unseemly side. Unfortunately, this doctrine of civilization is also central to Methodist statements on war.

## METHODISM, CIVILIZATION, AND WAR

In 1934 the Methodist Episcopal Church South developed an official position on war. The bishops addressed the problem of war in their Episcopal Address:

> War is another enemy to the human race which should no longer be tolerated by an intelligent, conscientious, honorable people. It is archaic, belongs to the jungle period of

---

24. Bowne, *The Principles of Ethics*, p. 284.
25. Paul Minus, *Walter Rauschenbusch: American Reformer* (New York: Macmillan, 1988), p. 105.

human development, and should be branded as an iniquitous and inhuman procedure.[26]

The bishops employ Bowne's doctrine of civilization wholeheartedly. War "should *no longer* be tolerated" — implying that before we reached this standard of human development it was at least tolerable, if not necessary.

The Committee on Temperance and Social Service received nine petitions on the subject of war and peace at the 1934 General Conference. They expanded upon a 1930 statement that suggested that war was allowable "only in the defense of those national ideals for the preservation of which the Republic was organized."[27] And the 1934 General Conference officially endorsed conscientious objection. This endorsement represented the official stance of the Methodist Episcopal Church South from 1934 till the Uniting Conference of 1939:

> The Methodist Episcopal Church, South, true to the principles of the New Testament, teaches respect for properly constituted civil authority. It holds that government rests upon the support of its conscientious citizenship, and that conscientious objectors to war in any or all of its manifestations are a natural outgrowth of the principle of good will and the Christian desire for universal peace; and that such objectors should not be oppressed by compulsory military service anywhere or at any time. We ask and claim exemption from all forms of military preparation or service for all conscientious objectors who may be members of the Methodist Episcopal Church, South. In this they have the authority and support of their Church.[28]

26. Journal of the Twenty-Second General Conference, Methodist Episcopal Church South (Nashville: The Methodist Publishing House, 1934), p. 367.

27. Ibid., p. 150.

28. *Book of Discipline of the Methodist Episcopal Church South* (Nashville: The Methodist Publishing House, 1934), par. 594.

This is one of the most intelligible statements on war found in the *Discipline* in the twentieth century. It refuses to make any unequivocal claims that it is unwilling to embody. Thus it has an honesty to it that is refreshing. It also suggests that the burden of proof does not rest on those who object to participation in the military, and so they have the full support of their church. But once again the basis for allowing conscientious objection has nothing to do with theological convictions; it has to do with political philosophy. Democratic government is based on the supposed consent of the governed. Therefore to disallow conscientious objection for the purpose of defending the government is to violate the basis of the government itself.[29]

The year 1939 was eventful for Methodism as the various branches of the Methodist Church were reunited. World War II had begun in Europe, and the question of whether the United States would enter the war was on everyone's mind. Taking as its theme the doctrine of civilization, the 1939 Uniting Conference adopted the following statement:

> *Whereas*, in the present extremely dangerous state of affairs existing among the nations of the world it is imperative that every possible influence looking toward the establishment of universal peace be asserted by the followers of the Prince of Peace; and,
> *Whereas*, a reunited and powerful Church is just now coming into existence whose voice in this grave situation ought to be unequivocal; and,
> *Whereas*, there exists an honest difference of opinion in regard to the particular form which the conviction of that Church in this crucial issue ought to take; therefore, be it
> *Resolved*, That The Methodist Church

29. The 1934 General Conference also required pastors "To preach at least once each year on world peace, the evils of war, and the evils attendant upon compulsory military training in schools and colleges." This is a remarkable testimony to their faithfulness — and it far surpasses the current practices in our schools and colleges.

1. Takes its stand undivided in its opposition to the spirit of war now raging through the world;

2. Pledges itself to exert every possible influence at its command to persuade belligerent people to find such ground of settlement of their difficulties as shall result in lasting peace between them;

3. Urges the President and the Congress of the United States to take every possible step to avoid the entanglement of our country in a world-wide conflagration of war which we are convinced would bring our civilization into ruins; and

4. Commits to our Board of Education the responsibility of laying the foundation of a system of Christian education which shall seek to eradicate the causes of war and train our children for Christian participation in the arts of peace.[30]

Once again we find the doctrine of civilization. War will "bring *our civilization* into ruins," and thus war threatens our self-understanding. War threatened the civilization that the church desired to defend.

The 1939 Uniting Conference made certain that all would realize what civilization they desired to protect. Directly before the "statement on peace and war" came this description of "our civilization":

> We cherish the freedom secured to mankind by this republic as among our own and the human race's most precious possessions. Political liberty is indeed nothing less than a necessary fruition of the gospel of Jesus Christ: so that devotion to it must, of course, command the Christian's utmost

30. *Book of Discipline of the Methodist Church* (Nashville: The Methodist Publishing House, 1939), p. 698. Notice the power of that last statement. While I am focusing on the problem of the poor theological basis for these statements — the doctrine of civilization — I do not want this focus to take away from the remarkable witness of these people. This call to train our children for peace is a powerful witness to their faithfulness, and it shows that their intended practice was much better than their theology.

resource, being conditioned only by that loyalty to the Living God Himself, by which alone free government can either be, or be made strong.

Being thus exalted and blessed in this liberty of Christian men and Americans, reunited Methodism publishes anew its thanksgiving for the great republic of the West; and pledges its devotion, its sacrifice, and its unceasing prayers that this high heritage received from our fathers be preserved for our children, and our children's children; and not only as undiminished, but as increased as in each advancing decade made more nobly fair.

Ponder this passage. It sacralizes America and claims that Methodists are willing to pledge their devotion to it and to sacrifice for it. What could this sacrifice imply other than being willing to fight, kill, and die? It commits Methodists to the "preservation" of this "freedom." And freedom is understood here as the absence of external constraints.

But this is not how Christians should understand "freedom." Christians believe that freedom does not occur when the will has no constraints, but only when the will is constrained by God's reconciling purposes. Thus the statement's view of freedom is opposed to the freedom defined by the journey of faith. To the credit of the statement, it does suggest that our loyalty to America is qualified by our "loyalty to the Living God Himself." But even though the Uniting Conference did understand allegiance to America as competing with allegiance to God, it still issued this statement.

How could a statement opposed to war follow directly after this call to sacrifice for America and pledge it our devotion? Only because these people were convinced that the best way to preserve "our civilization" was through pacifism. Pacifism was viewed not as a faithful following of Jesus, but as a necessary strategy to preserve the nation.

But what if the "barbarians" have not all been conquered and this rational and peaceful civilization is suddenly threatened? In the face of the increasing probability that the United States would enter the war, the General Conference of 1940 issued a statement that equivocates on the "undivided" stance of the 1939 statement:

> . . . we stand upon this ground: The Methodist Church, although making no attempt to bind the consciences of its individual members, will not officially endorse, support, or participate in war. We insist that the agencies of the Church shall not be used in preparation for war, but in the promulgation of peace. We insist that the buildings of the Church dedicated to the worship of God shall be used for that holy purpose, and not by any agency for the promotion of war.
>
> We have to recognize the fact that there is now no common judgment among Christians as to what a Christian should do when his own nation becomes involved in war. On this issue our own membership is divided. We believe, however, that the Christian Church, in a world torn asunder by bitter conflict, must not permit itself to be divided over any matter as to which it is possible for Christians sincerely to differ. We subscribe to this declaration of the Oxford Conference: "Recognizing that its members are called to live within the secular state or nation, and that in the event of war a conflict of duties is inevitable, [the Church] should help them to discover God's will, should then honor their conscientious decisions, whether they are led to participate in or to abstain from war, and maintain with both alike the full fellowship of the body of Christ. It should call upon them to repent and to seek together that deliverance from the entangling evil which can be found in Christ alone."
>
> Believing that "in the long run any people have far more to gain by cherishing freedom of conscience than by any regimentation that takes away that freedom" and that conscientious objection to war is a natural outgrowth of Christian desire for peace on earth, we ask and claim exemption from all forms of military preparation or service for all conscientious objectors who may be members of the Methodist Church. Those of our members who, as conscientious objectors, seek exemption from military training in schools and

colleges or from military service anywhere or at any time have the authority and support of their Church.[31]

And what if the "barbarians" are more of a threat than expected? The General Conference of 1944 issued a statement that is the exact opposite of the "undivided stance" of the 1939 statement — though still based on the same doctrine of civilization:

> As members of a church with world-wide relationships, we must remember that our deepest responsibility is to speak the truth. We must be willing to face the stern judgment of God upon evils in our own national life. By the same token we speak unequivocally regarding the *attack upon civilization* which has been made by the forces of aggression.
>
> In this country we are sending over a million young men from Methodist homes to participate in the conflict. God himself has a stake in the struggle, and he will uphold them as they fight forces destructive of the moral life of man. In Christ's name we ask for the blessing of God upon the men in the armed forces, and we pray for victory. We repudiate the theory that a state, even though imperfect in itself, must not fight against intolerable wrongs.
>
> While we respect the individual conscience of those who believe that they cannot condone the use of force, and staunchly will defend them on this issue, we cannot accept their position as the defining position of the Christian Church. We are well within the Christian position when we assert the necessity of the use of military forces to resist an aggression which would overthrow *every right which is held sacred by civilized men*.[32]

These statements of the Methodist General Conference thus moved from "undivided" opposition to war to affirmation of a "conscientious decision" to participate in war. While the 1940

31. *Book of Discipline of the Methodist Church* (Nashville: The Methodist Publishing House, 1940), pp. 777-78.
32. *Book of Discipline of the Methodist Church* (Nashville: The Methodist Publishing House, 1944), pp. 574-75; emphasis added.

resolution still placed the burden of proof on those who choose to fight, the 1944 statement actually endorsed those who fight and even claimed that "God himself has a stake in the struggle," suggesting that God's kingdom is now dependent upon our military capability. That is idolatry.

What is continuous through all of these transitions is the theme of the doctrine of civilization — the notion that the highest good is to place no external restraints on individual conscience. Freedom of individual conscience is central to the belief that our civilized form of government is based on the consent of the governed. Thus we cannot force anyone to fight or not to fight, and we must always make allowances for those who conscientiously disagree with us. What shifts in these three statements is who holds the burden of proof.

Ponder this unusual phrase from the 1940 statement: "The Methodist Church, although making no attempt to bind the consciences of its individual members, will not officially endorse, support, or participate in war." What does it mean for a church to "not officially endorse, support, or participate in war," while at the same time refusing to "bind the consciences of its individual members"? What understanding of the "official church" rejects requiring "individual members" to live out its convictions?

The 1944 statement is more honest: "While we respect the individual conscience of those who believe that they cannot condone the use of force, and staunchly will defend them on this issue, we cannot accept their position as the defining position of the Christian Church." Of course, such respect is extremely paternalistic toward pacifists, and the claim that the church "staunchly will defend them" neutralizes their position completely. In essence the statement implies that pacifists are wrong, but the church is willing to kill other people to defend their individual right to be wrong. This is one of the most insidious and demonic forms of hegemonic power there is.

The 1944 statement is more honest, but it is also a form of totalitarianism. The pacifist position is obliterated because of the doctrine of civilization. The warriors impose their will on the

pacifists and then refuse to confess that they have in fact constrained the pacifists by claiming to tolerate their position. But
their position is only tolerated insofar as it is rejected. The pacifists
are first "repudiated" — "we repudiate the theory that a state,
even though imperfect in itself, must not fight against intolerable
wrongs" — and then they are merely tolerated: "While we respect
the individual conscience of those who believe that they cannot
condone the use of force, and staunchly will defend them on this
issue, we cannot accept their position as the defining position of
the Christian Church." What kind of respect is based on complete
rejection? Freedom of individual conscience is only a smoke
screen to make the warriors' position more palatable.

What could "freedom of individual conscience" actually
mean with respect to what is required of church members? This
phrase is by no means self-interpreting, yet we will see that this
phrase remains foundational in the *Discipline* even to the present
day. In the statements on war, it means that individual
Methodists are not bound by the church's "undivided stance,"
whether that stance prohibits or permits participation in war.
That is obviously a morally unsound and intellectually incoher-
ent interpretation. Interpreting "freedom of conscience" to mean
that every Methodist is allowed to do what he or she pleases
irrespective of what the United Methodist Church says cannot be
an acceptable position within Methodism. The "meaning of
membership" within the church prohibits such an interpretation:

> When persons unite with a local United Methodist church,
> they profess their faith in God, the Father Almighty, maker
> of heaven and earth, and in Jesus Christ his only Son, and
> in the Holy Spirit. They covenant together with God and
> with the members of the local church to keep the vows which
> are a part of the order of confirmation and reception into the
> Church.[33]

33. *Book of Discipline*, par. 211.

The four vows that follow do not contain any explicit reference to whether Christians should or should not participate in war, but they do clearly suggest that individual members cannot simply do as they please according to the sanctity of their own individual conscience. The four vows are marked by language that emphasizes confessing, receiving, professing, promising, and being loyal. This language does not allow us to interpret "freedom of conscience" as freedom from having one's conscience bound by the church. Thus statements that honor individual conscience based on the doctrine of civilization are in contradiction with our understanding of church membership.

Another possible interpretation of "freedom of conscience" particularizes freedom of conscience to the issue of participation in war. While Methodist people are to be bound in conscience by the four vows, participation in war is a much more ambiguous issue. Because we are unclear concerning the Christian position on warfare, we allow a certain diversity based on a conscientious searching of the matter. This understanding of freedom of conscience is more palatable than the first. However, we must be extremely cautious that "ambiguity" does not become a safe haven from necessary and controversial stances. If we allow freedom of dissent from official church teaching due to ambiguity, then as we gain clarity we must narrow the dissent. And remember that in both the 1939 opposition to war and the 1944 endorsement of it, we did not offer ambiguous positions but unequivocal ones.

The 1940 General Conference statement reveals the breakdown of the liberal consensus that the best way to preserve "our civilization" is through pacifist strategies. A real threat to "our civilization" appeared that challenged the usefulness of pacifism as a strategy. Pacifism was still supposedly tolerated, but this appearance of toleration was based on the doctrine of civilization and its insistence on "freedom of conscience." Support was extended to conscientious objectors, not because this is an important aspect of Christian theology, but because diversity of opinion and freedom of conscience were necessary for "our civilization." Both the 1939 stance against war and the 1944 stance for war were based on the same doctrinal theme — the preservation of our civilization and the maintenance of freedom of conscience. And this theme is a discipline that binds the conscience of the Methodist people. Thus, by its very nature it is a contradiction!

Disciplining people into the doctrine of civilization neutralizes any theological account of pacifism and shapes all the disciplinary statements to come. As we have seen, the philosophical idea of "freedom of conscience" provides more of the foundation for Methodist statements concerning participation in war than does Methodist theology. Because the basis for the Methodist stance is "our civilization" rather than a tradition of Wesleyan theology, the Methodist Church was unable to stand against the spirit of war when it did in fact threaten "our civilization" in World War II.

My argument in this chapter has not been that Methodists have no discipline; indeed, they have a rigid and very effective discipline. Methodism has disciplined its people to preserve "our civilization," which is primarily defined as securing individual conscience against all external constraints. Of course, this discipline is itself an external constraint, but unfortunately, because it takes the form of insistence on freedom of individual conscience, this fact is seldom realized. Thus we have a contradictory theology that disciplines people against all discipline. This is what has led us to the ironic twist that our ability to discipline our members into the doctrine of civilization in this century is precisely what prevents us from disciplining them into faithful Christian discipleship. To accomplish the latter, we need to provide a counter-discipline, a discipline that could be formed from resources within our own tradition. In the next chapter we examine such resources.

# CHAPTER THREE

## *A Wesleyan Social Gospel*

Chapter 2 narrated both Methodism's "unequivocal" opposition to and its "unequivocal" support for Christian participation in war during the early part of the twentieth century. These contradictory unequivocal stances were grounded in the same foundational standard — the doctrine of civilization. A vision of civilization that emphasized freedom of individual conscience became both the ground and the purpose of the Methodist discipline. In 1972, when the United Methodist Church developed more fully its official stance on war, these earlier statements were so obviously opposed to each other that this purpose should have been called into question. Unfortunately, it was not. Instead, the United Methodist Church chose to live with contradictory claims.

The 1972 General Conference was important because it offered commentary on established standards of doctrine that had long been neglected. The Social Principles, as well as the document known as "Our Theological Task," can be properly understood as an attempt to interpret the established standards of doctrine for the newly formed United Methodists. This attempt benefited the church in that the commentary sought a place for the Articles of Religion and our Confession of Faith. However, it also had the deleterious effect of subordinating these established standards to the commentary; in fact, the commentary often contradicted the standards. In the discussion on war in the Social Principles this is so obvious that it is embarrassing.

The United Methodist Church lists as one of the twenty-one necessary "responsibilities and duties of a pastor" that every pastor should counsel parishioners concerning military service and its alternatives. But the contradictory statements as to what pastors are actually to counsel prevents them from knowing what they should say to parishioners even if they actually choose to fulfill this duty.[1] Thus, unlike other listed duties that are central to the life of the parish — such as preaching the Word, celebrating the sacraments, and visiting the sick — the duty to counsel members concerning military service has had at most an incidental role in the Methodist pastorate. This discrepancy between the stated purpose of ministry and its actual practice reveals a deep problem in United Methodism's ethics of war and peace.

## THE CONTRADICTION

In 1972, the members of the Committee on the Social Principles adopted the following statement on war:

> We believe war is incompatible with the teachings and example of Christ. We therefore reject war as an instrument of national foreign policy and insist that the first moral duty of all nations is to resolve by peaceful means every dispute that arises between or among them; that human values must outweigh military claims as governments determine their

1. The relevant portion of the *Discipline* is par. 439: "The pastor(s) shall oversee the total ministry of the local church in its nurturing ministries and in fulfilling its mission of witness and service in the world . . . (i) To counsel with members of the church and community concerning military service and its alternatives."

priorities; that the militarization of society must be challenged and stopped; that the manufacture, sale, and deployment of armaments must be reduced and controlled; and that the production, possession, or use of nuclear weapons be condemned.[2]

This statement is in continuity with the constitutional stance of Article 16. United Methodism's position on war — "we believe war is incompatible with the teachings and example of Christ" — is affirmed both in the Confession of Faith and in the Social Principles. Behind that claim is the suggestion that Holy Scripture provides the basis for this stance. Thus, unless the United Methodist Church has decided that the Christian life does not require following the teachings and example of Christ found in Scripture, war appears to be ruled out as a possible option.

That this is the intention of the statement on war is clear from the notes on the debate of the committee that formulated the Social Principles.[3] During the 1972 debates, Paul Ramsey was a member of the committee. He suggested that the statement on war as it stands would place United Methodism in solidarity with the historic peace churches and make normative a pacifist stance. Ramsey disagreed with such a stance, so he suggested an amendment that would read: "War is *ultimately* incompatible with the teaching and example of Christ." This better expressed Ramsey's own theological position that until Christ finally consummates the kingdom, war is not completely outside faithful Christian living. Under the constraints of the just war tradition, Ramsey believed, Christians could participate in war without violating the teaching and example of Christ.[4] But Ramsey's amendment was defeated, and the

2. *Book of Discipline,* par. 75.c, p. 109.
3. The notes on the debate come from the pen of Paul Ramsey, who was a participant on the 1972 committee. Ramsey's notes can be found in the Ramsey Papers at Duke University's Perkins Library.
4. For the best account of Ramsey's own position see his *War and*

General Conference — the only group that speaks officially for the United Methodist Church — passed the statement as is: "we believe war is incompatible with the teaching and example of Christ." The statement has remained in the *Discipline* without qualification since 1972.

As Ramsey rightly noted, the official position of the United Methodist Church appears to be pacifism. But this is not the whole story. The Committee on the Social Principles adopted a statement on military service. The initial sentence of that statement continues to place United Methodism firmly in the pacifist tradition: "Though coercion, violence, and war are presently the ultimate sanctions in international relations, we reject them as incompatible with the gospel and spirit of Christ." This is strong language! We *reject* coercion, violence, and war because they are faithless according to the life and teaching of Jesus Christ. Surely this is the beginning of a consistent, normative position that rejects war. Yet this is a faulty suggestion, for the remainder of the statement on military participation is anything but pacifism:

> We support and extend the ministry of the Church to those persons who conscientiously oppose all war, or any particular war, and who therefore refuse to serve in the armed forces or to cooperate with systems of military conscription. We also support and extend the Church's ministry to those persons who conscientiously choose to serve in the armed forces or to accept alternative service.[5]

This is a very strange use of the term *conscientiously*. Certainly the church should extend its ministry to both sets of people, but this is a formal claim that needs fuller articulation. How do we extend the church's ministry? The way in which we

---

the *Christian Conscience* (Durham, NC: Duke University Press, 1961), and his *The Just War* (Lanham: University Press of America, 1983).

5. *Book of Discipline*, par. 74.g, p. 108.

extend the ministry of the church should be consonant with the teaching and example of Christ, and the opening sentence of the statement has already said that war is "incompatible with the gospel and spirit of Christ." Thus the claim that we *support* those who choose conscientiously to reject the example and teaching of Christ is utterly baffling.

If the statement had read that we extend the ministry of the church to those who in invincible ignorance choose to serve in the armed forces, it would then be consistent with other parts of our *Discipline*, but as it is it makes absolutely no sense. And thus it is difficult for honest people to take our statements seriously. Paul Ramsey recognized this, and even though he himself favored a just war position and not pacifism, he suggested that the sentence read, "We also support and extend the Church's ministry to those persons who *in erring conscience* choose to serve in the armed forces." Ramsey's amendment was defeated and the General Conference passed the statement as is.

## THE CONTRADICTION EXPLAINED

How can we understand the United Methodist statement on war when it couples the complete rejection and denunciation of war with the support of those who conscientiously choose to participate in war? How can we counsel members about military participation when we are given such unequivocal and equivocal statements in the same *Discipline*? Viewed irenically, this contradiction might reflect our open, pluralistic, catholic spirit; viewed polemically, it is a sign of apostasy, or dishonesty, or at least cowardice. Viewed rightly, the contradiction is a logical result of the contradictory nature of the doctrine of civilization, which has provided a foundation for Methodism for far too long.

## *Pluralism?*

We seek to be an open and inclusive church. Inclusivity is grounded in our constitution. Article 4 under division one states:

> The United Methodist Church is a part of the Church Universal, which is one Body in Christ. Therefore, all persons, without regard to race, color, national origin, or economic condition, shall be eligible to attend its worship services, to participate in its programs, and, when they take the appropriate vows, to be admitted into its membership in any local church in the connection.

This is an important constitutional article. Its presence in our constitution was necessary because of the practice of segregating all African American churches from white churches from 1939 to 1968 in what was known as the "Central Jurisdiction." This policy of segregation excluded people from the community of faith and thus violated a basic rule of our life together: no one who is willing to "take the appropriate vows" can be excluded from any local United Methodist church.

We seek to be an open and inclusive church because openness and inclusivity are essential elements of a faithful church. The church wants all people to be reconciled to it, to be reconciled with each other, and to be reconciled to God. Thus the exclusion of anyone is deeply troubling.

John Wesley's sermon "Catholic Spirit" sets a precedent for our inclusivity. He refused to discriminate on the basis of worship practices. Wesley wrote:

> And how shall we choose among so much variety [of worship practices]? No man can choose for or prescribe to another. But everyone must follow the dictates of his own conscience in simplicity and godly sincerity. He must be fully persuaded in his own mind, and then act according to the

best light he has. . . . I dare not therefore presume to impose
my mode of worship on another. I believe it is truly primitive
and apostolical. But my belief is no rule for another. I ask
not therefore of him with whom I would unite in love, "Are
you of my Church? Of my congregation? Do you receive the
same form of church government and allow the same church
officers with me?"[6]

Wesley's catholic spirit is a marvelous testimony to the importance of an inclusive and unified church. In one sense, it is a
pacifist testimony; up until Wesley's time, Europe was overrun
with bloodletting due to intolerance of divergent worship practices. People were killing people over forms of worship, and
Wesley thought that violated the love commandment.

Yet Wesley's "catholic spirit" should not be abstracted
from its historical context and made into a general principle
applicable to all situations and times. Wesley himself did not
accept just any form of worship, let alone use the principle of
the catholic spirit to say that in every matter of faith "everyone
must follow the dictates of his own conscience." While this
appears to be what the church says today concerning participation in war, such a position would be impossible in a church
founded on a theology of discipline with holiness as its purpose. Even in this sermon, Wesley refuses to accept the dictates
of a person's conscience without qualification. Thus he also
writes:

a catholic spirit is not *speculative latitudinarianism*. It is not an
indifference to all opinions. This is the spawn of hell, not the
offspring of heaven. This unsettledness of thought, this being
"driven to and fro, and tossed about with very wind of
doctrine", is a great curse, not a blessing; an irreconcilable
enemy, not a friend, to true catholicism. . . . a catholic spirit

6. "Catholic Spirit," in *The Works of John Wesley*, vol. 2, ed. Albert C.
Outler (Nashville: Abingdon Press, 1985), pp. 84-87.

is not any kind of *practical latitudinarianism*. It is not indifference as to public worship or as to the outward manner of performing it. This likewise would not be a blessing but a curse. Far from being an help thereto it would, so long as it remained, be an unspeakable hindrance to the worshipping of God in spirit and in truth. But the man of a truly catholic spirit, having weighed all things in the balance of the sanctuary, has no doubt, no scruple at all concerning that particular mode of worship wherein he joins. He is clearly convinced that *this* manner of worshipping God is both scriptural and rational.[7]

Wesley's "catholic spirit" referred to inclusivity regarding worship practices; it used a reasoned argument based on Scripture to evaluate forms of worship. It is not indifference to forms of worship, let alone indifference to such an important aspect of the Christian life as participation in warfare.

Indifference destroys the reconciling nature of the church just as much as exclusivity does. When "freedom of individual conscience" replaces the purpose of reconciliation, then openness and tolerance become ways in which we abandon people to themselves. We do not want to make difficult decisions that will affect other people's lives, so we leave them to decide for themselves how they will live. Once "freedom of individual conscience" becomes a dogmatic standard so that evaluations of faithfulness can no longer be made, then our contradictory statements suggest either apostasy, dishonesty, or cowardice. Remember that even our constitutional guarantee of inclusivity is restricted to those who "take the appropriate vows."

---

7. Ibid., pp. 92-93. "Latitudinarianism" refers to a movement whereby people reduce the form of worship to the lowest common denominator.

## *Apostasy?*

The statement of support for those who conscientiously choose not to follow Christ's example and teaching as defined in the *Discipline* could suggest that the United Methodist Church is indifferent to the activities of its members and thus that it seeks only a superficial latitudinarian unity. The contradiction between our unequivocal rejection of war as a faithful Scriptural response to following Jesus and our support of those who choose to participate in war could suggest that we do not believe that following the example and teaching of Christ is necessary for church membership. That is an odd statement for a church to make. In fact it is much more than odd; it is scandalous. It is a sign of an apostate church, and it is a good reason for anyone who believes that following Jesus is central to the Christian life to be done with the United Methodists immediately. However, judging the United Methodists' contradictory statements on war as apostasy would be a bit rash.[8] The "marks of membership" outlined in the *Discipline* suggest that United Methodism does believe that following the example and teaching of Jesus is necessary for church membership. These four marks of membership are:

1. To confess Jesus Christ as Lord and Savior and pledge allegiance to his Kingdom,

---

8. For a good discussion of apostasy, see Kenneth E. Kirk's *The Vision of God* (London: Longmans, Green, 1943), pp. 221-34. Traditionally it was believed that even apostasy could be overcome once; thus one repentance for apostasy after baptism was allowed. Here apostasy means that people recanted the faith when they were forced to do so by the ruling authority. The connection between our own claim that war is incompatible with the teaching and example of Christ and the recantation of that claim in face of military conscription does approach apostasy, but I do think that the analogy is overdrawn and thus our position resembles dishonesty or cowardice much more than apostasy.

71

2. To receive and profess the Christian faith as contained in the Scriptures of the Old and New Testaments,

3. To promise according to the grace given them to live a Christian life and always remain faithful members of Christ's holy Church,

4. And to be loyal to the United Methodist Church and uphold it by their prayers, their presence, their gifts and their service.[9]

Since this description of church membership clearly shows that the teachings and example of Jesus Christ are necessary for the people called Methodists, another reason needs to be found for the discrepancy between United Methodism's rejection of war and its unqualified support of those who participate in war.

## Dishonesty?

A third possible explanation is that United Methodists do not truly believe that war is incompatible with the teaching and example of Christ. Therefore, they are unwilling to require anyone to leave military service or to create a category for those who are related to the church but not yet willing to pledge their allegiance to Christ.[10]

While this explanation makes the discrepancy intelligible, it also means that the United Methodist Church is dishonest. Anyone with the slightest inkling of the moral life knows that

9. *Book of Discipline,* par. 211, pp. 124-25.

10. John Wesley had such a category. People who desired to follow Christ but were not yet capable of a commitment to do so were called "seekers"; they were allowed to participate in the class meetings with the hope that they would one day be enabled to make such a commitment. Such a category of church membership would be quite helpful today; it would make membership important and remind us that to call ourselves Christians is not such an easy thing to do.

when you say something you do not mean you are lying. Understanding the contradictory nature of our statements on war by way of dishonesty is not very satisfying. Yet the General Conference, the only group empowered to speak for all of those who call themselves United Methodists, claims both that "war is incompatible with the teaching and example of Christ" and that the church will support all those who reject this claim. While dishonesty may be a better explanation than apostasy, it still remains unacceptable.

## Cowardice?

Perhaps the contradictory statements on war were not the result of a simple case of dishonesty. Perhaps the people who passed the statements against war — the members of the Committee on the Social Principles and the members of the 1972 General Conference and every General Conference since then — truly did believe that war is incompatible with the teaching and example of Christ, but they were unwilling to request the rest of the church to live out their convictions.[11] If so, the statement that we will support those who choose to violate Christ's teaching by participating in the military service was a concession to those who disagreed with the position. This betokens neither apostasy nor dishonesty but cowardice. Allowances can certainly be made by the church for those who are not yet seeking to live out the teachings and example of Christ, but to support

11. If this is the case, and I find this the most plausible explanation, it shows a glaring inconsistency in the General Conference. General Conferences have consistently suggested that a gay or lesbian life-style is also incompatible with the teaching and example of Christ, but in this case they have been willing to impose their conviction on the whole church. How do we make sense of this contradiction? Does not all of this betray a deep spiritual problem with the way theology is done by committee in United Methodism?

those who are unwilling to follow Christ's teachings because we do not want to offend them reveals that we do not have the strength of our convictions.

Moral virtues such as courage go hand in hand with intellectual virtues, and thus a lack of courage contributes to a lack of intellectual consistency. It is easy to see how cowardice in the church can lead to the kind of intellectual incoherence found in the United Methodist statements on war. If we do not have the strength of our convictions, we should expect that our convictions will not cohere intellectually. Thomas Aquinas knew this well, and our church would benefit from his wisdom.[12]

## The Sacredness of Freedom of Conscience

Apostasy, dishonesty, and cowardice are theological vices that prevent faithful participation in the example and teaching of Christ. These vices can be given no room in a believer's heart. If in fact the people called United Methodists believe that war is incompatible with the teaching and example of Christ, then they must provide ways in which military service is avoided by all people called Methodists. But there is an explanation of

12. See Thomas Aquinas, *Summa Theologica* 1a2ae, Question 58, "The Difference Between Moral and Intellectual Virtues." I am convinced that another central problem with our position on war is that we assume that our first task is to make "public policy," which involves only intellectual virtues of theoretical reasoning, and we neglect the moral virtues concomitant with the necessary exercise of practical reasoning. The latter would require some form of habituation within the church based on our positions against war. Paragraph 439.i of our *Discipline* requires such an exercise, but the implementation of public policy does not require any such habituation. Therefore our official statements are failing to provide something that paragraph 439.i requires: the moral habituation of the virtue of peace rooted in practical reasoning. Instead, all the church offers are intellectual exercises in theoretical reasoning.

the contradiction that avoids explaining it in terms of apostasy, dishonesty, or cowardice.

Unfortunately, while the *substance* of the disciplinary statements on war does not reflect the conviction of many Methodists, the *tolerance* of these irreconcilable, contradictory positions does. Therefore, the correct interpretation of this contradiction is that it is a logical result in a church that disciplines its members into the doctrine of civilization, holding individual conscience more sacred than anything else. This new foundational standard that usurps practical divinity makes the obvious contradiction appear perfectly logical — logical, but still not faithful.

Once the practice of disciplining members into this new standard took firm root in our church, mandates to counsel concerning military service lost an intelligible context. Without practical divinity and a theology of discipline that holds up holiness of heart and life — as defined by the story of Jesus and witnessed to by the stories of the saints — as the chief end of all of humanity, and without this holiness being the vision that binds laity and clergy together on a common journey, what reason do pastors have to engage parishioners in such a risky discussion? All they are left with is an endlessly open-ended discussion about war.

The faithful practice of the ministry cannot overlook the question of war and military participation, and such a question must have a context that permits more than an endlessly open-ended discussion based on each person's conscience; theological discussions of war need something more substantive to guide them. Such substance can be found within our own tradition in the theology of discipline. This theology of discipline allows us to develop a counter-discipline to the doctrine of civilization, enabling us to avoid the inevitable contradictions implied when individual conscience becomes the only standard for a people.

## OVERCOMING THE SELF
## THROUGH THE USE OF RULES

Theology is a social enterprise. The social nature of theology finds expression in the Wesleyan emphasis on discipline. Discipline requires that one's will be bound to a group of people on a journey from sin to holiness; without such discipline people are left to their own desires, and as George Bernard Shaw so aptly said, hell is where God gives you what you want. No single individual can authorize theology based on his or her own rational capacity. Yet in spite of this, early in the nineteenth century the individual's rational capacity became the standard for theological reflection in the school of personalism.

The very term *personalism* implied that the ultimate authority was the individual person. The individual person was the authority because, as Borden Parker Bowne stated, "The principles of knowing are primarily immanent laws of mental activity."[13] Because knowledge is primarily a function of categories in the individual's mind, right reasoning is only possible when those categories are free from all external restraints, particularly the external restraints imposed by ecclesiastical authority.

A. C. Knudsen stated that this was the genius of Borden Parker Bowne and of Boston personalism. Personalism overcame an "external and absolute authority" and released faith "from bondage alike to tradition and to reason."[14] Knudsen wrote:

> The reality of the soul or self or "I" is the fundamental presupposition of personalism; it is even a more characteristic doctrine than the existence of a personal God.[15]

13. Borden Parker Bowne, *Personalism* (Boston: Houghton Mifflin, 1908), p. 57.
14. A. C. Knudsen, *The Doctrine of God* (New York: Abingdon–Cokesbury Press, 1930), p. 80.
15. A. C. Knudsen, *The Philosophy of Personalism* (Boston: Boston University Press, 1949), p. 67.

Thus Knudsen claimed that "the mind must be its own judge."[16] Any ecclesiastical authority that set itself up as judge would deny this fundamental tenet.

> Our faculties do not operate automatically in the sense that they necessarily lead to truth; this would deny the fact of error. They need to be guided by a standard immanent within them, and this guidance is possible only on the assumption that the human spirit is free. Freedom is, therefore, necessary to the trustworthiness of reason; without it there would be no way of accounting for error.[17]

Given this, it is an ironic twist of Methodist history that the majority of ecclesiastical authorities in the twentieth century were trained as Boston personalists. The notion of "freedom of individual conscience" became a dogma that Methodist institutions autocratically demanded of all their members. This should cause us to suspect that the "freedom" asserted here functioned not so much as a criticism of institutional authority, but as a way in which authority could be deceptively embedded in Methodism so that it could not be challenged.

More important than the deceptive way in which Boston personalism was used to entrench an unquestioned institutional authority is the way in which the fundamental tenet of the freedom of the individual destroyed the Wesleyan understanding of discipline as a central theological category. The theology of discipline, because it is by nature a social enterprise, cannot exist in an environment where the final authority is the individual self. The authority for our theological reflection must shift away from the individual if we are to recover a theology of discipline.

Wesley understood the importance of discipline. His

16. Ibid., p. 143.
17. Ibid., p. 149.

class meeting was a new way of embodying the practice of "binding and loosing" in continuity with traditional penitential practices. This is readily seen in Wesley's use of "rules," standards used to measure the health of the covenant community. For this purpose the "General Rules of the Methodist Church" were developed. These general rules are enforced by the restrictive rules, which were set down in 1808 as the one source of authority in the Methodist Church that cannot be changed by the General Conference. The fifth restrictive rule protects the general rules from any future tampering: "The General Conference shall not revoke or change the General Rules of Our United Societies."[18] Every member of the Methodist Church is bound by the restrictions imposed through the restrictive rules.

Basically, we have three general rules: Methodists must (1) do no harm, "by avoiding evil of every kind"; (2) do good, "by being in every kind merciful after their power; as they have opportunity, doing good of every possible sort"; and (3) attend "upon all the ordinances of God."[19] These three general rules are then developed more fully; for instance, doing no harm includes abstention from

> Slaveholding; buying or selling slaves.
> Fighting, quarreling, brawling, brother going to law with brother; returning evil for evil, or railing for railing; the using of many words in buying or selling.
> The buying or selling goods that have not paid the duty.
> The giving or taking of things on usury — that is, unlawful interest.

Included under the second general rule is the mandate to do good by doing the following:

18. *Book of Discipline,* par. 19, p. 26.
19. *Book of Discipline,* par. 68.

To their bodies, of the ability which God giveth, by giving food to the hungry, by clothing the naked, by visiting or helping them that are sick or in prison. . . .

By all possible diligence and frugality, that the gospel be not blamed.

By running with patience the race which is set before them, denying themselves, and taking up their cross daily; submitting to bear the reproach of Christ, to be as the filth and offscouring of the world; and looking that men should say all manner of evil of them *falsely*, for the Lord's sake.

And finally, under the third general rule, attendance of the following is required:

The public worship of God.
The ministry of the Word, either read or expounded.
The Supper of the Lord.
Family and private prayer.
Searching the Scriptures.
Fasting or abstinence.[20]

These general rules provide a framework within which Methodist theological reflection is to occur. They are filled with great insights into the nature of our journey in faith. Recovering them would be helpful in each of our lives, but you cannot recover the rules simply by applying them in a rigorous and rigid fashion. Questions need to be asked about the meaning of each rule, and interpretations must be offered. For instance, the rule against slaveholding obviously seems dated. But what about the economic practices of many Methodists today — for example, large farmers who employ migrant farmworkers to work their fields because it is economically advantageous? This practice has a direct connection with the practice of slavery,

20. Ibid.

and the practices of these farmers affect the witness of all who are Methodists. Do not such practices result in outsiders blaming the gospel for our inability to live out our own rules? And similar questions can be asked about each of the other rules. For example, what constitutes usurious practices? How does our usury prevent us from making a faithful witness?

This brings us to a crucial point in the theology of discipline. The general rules are to be used for the purpose of ordering our lives so that we might be able to proclaim the gospel with integrity. The gospel transforms people's lives; it is not a ritualistic solvent to dilute our consciences, but a power of righteousness. Through the gospel we are taken up into the obedience of Christ and we actually participate in the Triune Life. Our participation is our salvation. Because we participate in the Trinity, salvation brings not only justification but also sanctification. The general rules structure our life together for our participation in sanctification.

## GOING ON TO PERFECTION

Wesley believed that the Christian life does not simply "impute" righteousness to Christians. That is to say, we are not saved without also being transformed and having the righteousness of Christ work a true change in our lives. This is why he coupled the doctrine of justification with the doctrine of sanctification. Justification implies that our sins are forgiven without any effort on our part. This is God's gracious act of "imputed" righteousness. But once our sins are forgiven, then the Holy Spirit begins a work of "inherent righteousness" within us. This constitutes our sanctification and sets us out on the journey toward perfection.

Justification without sanctification leads to a cheap form of grace that cannot save. In a sermon called "The Lord Our

Righteousness," Wesley rhetorically asked himself the question "But do not you believe *inherent* righteousness?" He responded:

> Yes, in its proper place; not as the *ground* of our acceptance with God, but as the *fruit* of it; not in the place of *imputed* righteousness, but as consequent upon it. That is, I believe God *implants* righteousness in every one to whom he has *imputed* it.[21]

Why is Wesley so concerned with "inherent righteousness"? He explains later in this sermon:

> In the meantime what we are afraid of is this: lest any should use the phrase, "the righteousness of Christ", or, "the righteousness of Christ is 'imputed to me'," as a cover for his unrighteousness. We have known this done a thousand times. A man has been reproved, suppose, for drunkenness. "Oh, said he, I pretend to no righteousness of *my own*: Christ is *my righteousness*." Another has been told that "the extortioner, the unjust, shall not inherit the kingdom of God." He replies with all assurance, "I am unjust in myself, but I have a spotless righteousness in Christ." And thus though a man be as far from the practice as from the tempers of a Christian, though he neither has the mind which was in Christ nor in any respect walks as he walked, yet he has armour of proof against all conviction in what he calls the "righteousness of Christ."[22]

Wesley rejects any theology that assumes that God does not work an actual righteousness in our lives.

The Christian faith is not only about the forgiveness of our sins; it is also about the gracious possibility of turning from sin to holiness of life. Wesley is adamant that this be understood and preached by the people called Methodists:

21. "The Lord Our Righteousness," in *The Works of John Wesley,* vol. 1, ed. Albert C. Outler (Nashville: Abingdon Press, 1984), p. 458.
22. Ibid., p. 462.

O warn them (it may be they will hear *your* voice) against "continuing in sin that grace may abound"! Warn them against making "Christ the minister of sin"! Against making void that solemn decree of God, "without holiness no man shall see the Lord," by a vain imagination of being *holy in Christ.* O warn them that if they remain unrighteous, the righteousness of Christ will profit them nothing! Cry aloud (is there not a cause?) that for this very end the righteousness of Christ is imputed to us, that "the righteousness of the law may be fulfilled in us," and that we may "live soberly, religiously, and godly in this present world."[23]

That last sentence is important. Wesley emphasizes that the purpose for the imputed righteousness of Christ is that the law may be *fulfilled in us.* In language similar to that of Article 16 of our Confession of Faith, which suggests that we owe the state "sober, righteous, and godly" obedience but not participation in violence and warfare, Wesley understands that the purpose of the "law" is that we might live "*soberly, religiously, and godly* in the present world." This is our mission. It is how we serve the present age.

Why should you be concerned about an eighteenth-century discussion of imputed and inherent righteousness in a sermon by the folk theologian, John Wesley? If you are not Methodist or are not concerned with the Methodist tradition, then you need not be, unless you desire out of sisterly concern to keep Methodists faithful to the best of their own tradition. But if you were baptized in the Methodist Church, and you desire to take seriously the vows you made (or that were made on your behalf), then the sermons have a certain authority over your life. They "function as the traditional standard exposition of distinctive Methodist teaching."[24] Unlike the Articles of Religion, they do not have the force of

23. Ibid., p. 463.
24. *Book of Discipline,* par. 67, p. 54.

church law behind them, but they do carry the weight of tradition.[25]

Tradition does not imply a rigid and inviolable connection with the past; rather, tradition is a reading of our past that helps us make sense of who we are in the present. Wesley's sermons are important for us because they represent an ongoing conversation about who we are. If we have come to a point where we now believe sin is inevitable and that we must "sin boldly," then we need to be honest and realize that this represents a decisive theological shift away from Wesley. Such shifts are possible within a tradition, but this is one shift I think Methodists would be ill advised to tolerate. Neither should we tolerate the shift away from coupling justification with sanctification to emphasizing justification alone, because this cheapens grace. If we believe that something is sin — that is to say, if we believe it to be contrary to the gospel and spirit of Christ — then it cannot be tolerated among us except as we wait upon the Lord to rid us of it.

Since 1968 we have had a constitutional stance that says that war is sin. Despite this stance, we still tolerate the practice of war among our people. In doing so, we have shifted our theology away from Wesley's understanding of the inseparable connection between justification and sanctification and have, in practice, severed the two. To allow Methodists to continue to participate in war even after war has been named sinful shows that we have left Wesley and his sermons behind, rejecting — without debate — an important part of who we are.

Of course, astute readers will be wondering how I can recover Wesley to support a pacifist position when he himself was not a pacifist but held to the just war article found in the Anglican Articles of Religion. My response is twofold. First, Wesley was not confronted in his church discipline, as we are,

25. For a fuller discussion of this see Thomas A. Langford, ed., *Doctrine and Theology in the United Methodist Church* (Nashville: Abingdon Press, 1991).

with a tradition that says that war is sin. He was an Anglican; we are United Methodists. The "United" is important, for our tradition was formed through the merging of the Evangelical United Brethren and Methodist traditions. Thus the problem did not arise for Wesley in the same way that it does for us. If Wesley did not understand war to be sin, then from within our own tradition we can claim that Wesley was wrong.

Yet Wesley does seem to suggest in many places that war is problematic for Christians. For instance, in "Sermon on the Mount, III" he writes:

> we may easily learn in how wide a sense the term "peacemakers" is to be understood. In its literal meaning it implies those lovers of God and man who utterly detest and abhor all strife and debate, all variance and contention; and accordingly labour with all their might either to prevent this fire of hell from being kindled, or when it is kindled from breaking out, or when it is broke out from spreading any farther. They endeavour to calm the stormy spirits of men, to quiet their turbulent passions, to soften the minds of contending parties, and if possible reconcile them to each other. They use all innocent arts, and employ all their strength, all the talents which God has given them, as well to preserve peace where it is as to restore it where it is not.[26]

This does not sound like the rhetoric of just war, for Wesley speaks only of "innocent arts." He makes no concessions to war in this sermon, even though he does make such concessions in other places.[27]

---

26. "Sermon on the Mount, III," in Outler, ed., *The Works of John Wesley*, vol. 1, pp. 517-18.

27. See Brian Turley's "John Wesley and War," *Methodist History* 29, 2 (1991), for an essay that applies the just war categories to Wesley. Turley's essay is helpful, but he anachronistically assumes that Wesley's just war position was more consistent than is plausible for an eighteenth-century thinker.

Whatever Wesley's own position, since 1968 our church has had a tradition that identifies war as sin. We also have a tradition that says that Christianity is not simply about forgiveness of sins, but also about the overcoming of sin through the process of sanctification. The convergence of these two traditions leads me to believe that faithfulness to our tradition requires our church to take a bold stance by refusing, at every level, to participate in war.

My second response to the objection that Wesley himself took a just war stance rather than a pacifist stance is that the church should always make room for a just war position *at the outer limits of faithful Christian living.*[28]

These two responses explain the way in which I want to recover Wesley's theology of discipline as central to the Methodist Church and use that theology to call the church into a stance that refuses participation in war. This means that we take Wesley's understanding of the function of the law seriously. The General Rules are a theological expression in our polity of Wesley's use of the law.

Remember that in emphasizing sanctification Wesley stated that the "very end" — that is, the purpose — of justification is not simply that our sins be forgiven, but that "the righteousness of the law may be fulfilled in us." When we claim that war is contrary to the spirit and gospel of Christ, but do not expect people to respond by refusing to participate in war, we understand justification only as imputation of righteousness and neglect the sanctifying grace that works the righteousness of the law within us.

28. Obviously this needs further explanation. How can I call on the church to refuse to cooperate in war while at the same time allowing for a just war position at all? The answer to this contradiction lies in the fact that I understand the just war teaching as a therapy to heal our souls from a warlike spirit. Thus it is a penitential practice to reconcile back into the church those who still feel compelled through reasons of political expediency to fight in wars. The purpose of the rules forged out for just war is to show Christians the only possible exception that can be found to our refusal to participate in war. This will be discussed further in the next chapter.

This understanding of theology is much more like that of the influential theologian Reinhold Niebuhr than like that of John Wesley. In a famous essay called "Why the Christian Church Is Not Pacifist," Niebuhr wrote:

> The good news of the gospel is not the law that we ought to love one another. The good news of the gospel is that there is a resource of divine mercy which is able to overcome a contradiction within our souls, which we cannot ourselves overcome. This contradiction is that, though we know we ought to love our neighbor as ourself, there is a "law in our members which wars against the law that is in our mind" (Rom. 7:23), so that, in fact, we love ourselves more than our neighbor.
>
> The grace of God which is revealed in Christ is regarded by Christian faith as, on the one hand, an actual "power of righteousness" which heals the contradiction within our hearts. In that sense Christ defines the actual possibilities of human existence. On the other hand, this grace is conceived as "justification," as pardon rather than power, as the forgiveness of God, which is vouchsafed to man despite the fact that he never achieves the full measure of Christ. In that sense Christ is the "impossible possibility." Loyalty to him means realization in intention, but does not actually mean the full realization of the measure of Christ. In this doctrine of forgiveness and justification, Christianity measures the full seriousness of sin as a permanent factor in human history.[29]

Niebuhr's discussion of the law and the gospel differs greatly from Wesley's. Niebuhr does not suggest that the purpose of justification is the realization of the law of love in believers. Instead he insists that the purpose of justification is the overcoming of the contradiction that the law creates within us. The

---

29. "Why the Christian Church Is Not Pacifist," in *The Essential Reinhold Niebuhr*, ed. Robert McAfee Brown (New Haven: Yale University Press, 1986), pp. 102-3.

law convicts us of sin. This creates a contradiction in our souls that leads us to despair. The gospel heals the contradiction, but it does so primarily through forgiveness and not through an actual power of righteousness in the believer.

Niebuhr allows that an "actual 'power of righteousness' " does occur in the believer that is similar to Wesley's view of inherent righteousness, but Niebuhr places it only within "intention." Thus, unlike Wesley and the early Methodists, Niebuhr disallows the doctrine of perfection. God cannot actually make people holy. God can forgive sins, but sin is a "permanent factor in human history." The purpose of holiness is lost.

While Reinhold Niebuhr was one of the most influential theologians in the United States in the twentieth century, his theology is diametrically opposed to Methodism. If Niebuhr was right, then Wesley was — and is — wrong. Niebuhr's basic premise was that the contradiction between the law and the gospel cannot be eradicated. The law brings judgment and despair; the gospel heals the judgment and despair, but does not bring the ability to live oı t the law. We can never fully participate in the peaceable holiness of the Triune Life.

Niebuhr also disagrees with Wesley in that he individualizes Christianity. The gospel is applied to the contradiction within the individual's soul, not to any social order. Wesley, on the other hand, understood Christianity as essentially social. In "Sermon on the Mount, IV" he writes, "I shall endeavour to show that Christianity is essentially a social religion, and that to turn it into a solitary religion is indeed to destroy it." He goes on to explain what he means by a "social" religion. "When I say this is essentially a social religion, I mean not only that it cannot subsist so well, but that it cannot subsist at all without society, without living and conversing with other men."[30]

30. "Sermon on the Mount, IV," in Outler, ed., *The Works of John Wesley*, vol. 1, pp. 533-34.

Niebuhr understood the social order only in reference to the nation, and he thought it was impossible for the nation to live without sin. While this may or may not be true, Wesley understood the social element of Christianity to consist not in a nation but in a group of people bound together in the journey from sin to holiness, who in their sociality are able to be accountable to each other and to the Holy Spirit in such a way that sin could be overcome. In other words, the community of believers is the "social" element in Christianity. This journey from sin to holiness is not a sectarian journey; rather, it is a journey that requires conversation — both with other Christians and with non-Christians. Without such interaction, says Wesley, how could one live out the law of the gospel, which requires "mercifulness whereby 'we love our enemies, bless them that curse us, do good to them that hate us, and pray for them which despitefully use us and persecute us.' "[31]

## THE LAW

One of the necessary provisions for the journey from sin to holiness was "the law." In "Sermon on the Mount, V" Wesley has an interesting interpretation of the Pharisees. Rather than viewing the Pharisees as a group of legalistic hypocrites, he uses Jesus' denunciation of the Pharisees as an indictment upon Christians. When Jesus required that our righteousness exceed that of the scribes and Pharisees, he was not belittling them but instructing us. The Pharisees had a certain righteousness: they sought to do no harm, to do good, and to attend upon all the ordinances of God. As you can see, these are the three general principles Wesley includes in the General Rules; this is "the righteousness of a Pharisee," and Wesley applauds it.

31. Ibid., p. 536.

The Pharisees are not wrong because they are legalistic, but Christians are called to the righteousness of a Pharisee and then some. We are to do more. We are to internalize "holy tempers" and not be satisfied with the following of the rules themselves. While the rules are necessary, they are not an end in themselves; their purpose is to instill in us "holy tempers." These "holy tempers" include "poverty of spirit, mourning, meekness, hunger and thirst after righteousness, the love of our neighbour, and purity of heart, . . . peacemaking . . . and suffering for righteousness' sake."[32]

Unlike Niebuhr, Wesley refuses to set the law and the gospel in contradiction to each other. In fact, he insists

> that there is no contrariety at all between the law and the gospel; that there is no need for the law to pass away in order to the establishing of the gospel. Indeed neither of them supersedes the other, but they agree perfectly well together. Yea, the very same words, considered in different respects, are parts both of the law and of the gospel.[33]

Wesley's theology of discipline, with its insistence on the place of rules, is built upon this understanding of the law. If the purpose of the law is only to bring judgment and despair, then we understand the law only as it applies to us as sinners. This negative function of the law has its usefulness, but there is more to the purpose of the law than this. In asserting a more positive function of the law, Wesleyan theology rejects the kind of law and gospel themes that are found in Luther and that undergird the theology of Reinhold Niebuhr.

For Luther, the law has only two functions. Paul Althaus describes them thus:

32. "Sermon on the Mount, V," in Outler, ed., *The Works of John Wesley*, vol. 1, p. 568.
33. Ibid., p. 554.

The first function of the law is to hinder gross transgressions and crimes in this world of sin which is controlled by the devil. It thus preserves public peace and makes possible the education of the young and, particularly, the preaching of the gospel. The law does this in the form of the God-instituted offices of government, parents, and teachers, as well as through the civil laws. . . .

The law has a second function insofar as it is not simply understood in its civil or in its "political" sense but also in its spiritual sense; and this latter is its true and genuine meaning. . . . sinful man . . . cannot fulfill [the law]. . . . It constantly accuses him and delivers him up to God's wrath, to judgment, and to eternal death. This is the law's power. . . . It intends to, and actually does, awaken men out of their unawareness, make them feel the power of the law, recognize their sin, experience God's wrath, and be led to repentance.[34]

For Luther, since the fall, the law cannot be fulfilled. It only leads people to repentance and convicts them of sin.

After Luther, Lutheran orthodoxy expanded Luther's twofold use of the law to a fourfold use:

1. *The political use of the Law* consists in the preservation of external discipline.
2. The *elenchtical* use consists in the manifestation and reproof of sins, but also in the demonstration of the most severe divine judgments.
3. *The pedagogic use* of the Law consists in indirectly compelling the sinner to go to Christ.
4. *The didactic use* consists in the instruction and direction of all internal and external moral actions.[35]

34. Paul Althaus, *The Theology of Martin Luther* (Philadelphia: Fortress Press, 1966), pp. 253-55. I am indebted to Brent Laytham for this quote.
35. Heinrich Schmid, ed., *The Doctrinal Theology of the Evangelical*

This expanded understanding of the law's functions did not develop a positive usage; for Luther and Lutheran orthodoxy, the law cannot be fulfilled. Since the fall, the law and the gospel are contrary, never again to be joined this side of the eschaton. The law can only function negatively, either by convicting people of sin and thus leading them to Christ, or by restraining evildoers through political force and coercion.

John Calvin also developed a law-gospel theology, but he gave the law a more positive twist. His first two functions of the law are similar to Luther's, but he also noted a third, more positive function of the law. Calvin's three uses of the law are as follows:

> The first part is this: while it shows God's righteousness, that is, the righteousness alone acceptable to God, it warns, informs, convicts, and lastly condemns, every man of his own unrighteousness.[36]

> The second function of the law is this: at least by fear of punishment to restrain certain men who are untouched by any care for what is just and right unless compelled by hearing the dire threats in the law.[37]

> The third and principal use, which pertains more closely to the proper purpose of this law, finds its place among believers in whose hearts the Spirit of God already lives and reigns.[38]

Calvin explains this "third and principal use" more fully. Christians "profit" from the law positively in two ways. First, the

---

*Lutheran Church*, trans. Charles A. Hay and Henry E. Jacobs (Philadelphia: The United Lutheran Publishing House, 1899), pp. 515-16. This source, as well as the original idea for much of this discussion of the law, comes from a footnote in Outler, ed., *The Works of John Wesley*, vol. 2, p. 15.

36. John Calvin, *Institutes of the Christian Religion*, ed. John T. McNeill (Philadelphia: Westminster Press, 1960), 2.7, vol. 1, p. 354.

37. Ibid., p. 358.

38. Ibid., p. 360.

law allows them to understand the nature of the divine will better: "Here is the best instrument for them to learn more thoroughly each day the nature of the Lord's will to which they aspire, and to confirm them in the understanding of it." Second, the law functions positively by drawing believers "back from the slippery path of transgression."[39]

Wesley followed Calvin in stating that the law has three functions, but he emphasized the positive sense even more than Calvin did; he also diminished the negative sense of the political function found in both Calvin and Luther.

> [T]he first use of [the law], without question, is to convince the world of sin. This is indeed the peculiar work of the Holy Ghost who can work it without any means at all, or by whatever means it pleaseth him. . . . But it is the ordinary method of the Spirit of God to convict sinners by the law.[40]

This first use of the law is basically identical with Calvin and Luther: the law convicts people of sin.

But Wesley's second function is strikingly different from both Luther and Calvin. For both of them, the second function of law provides the political authorities with permission to coerce people who have malicious intentions in order to restrain their evil ways. Wesley's second function has nothing to do with that restraining function of the law. Instead, he states:

> The second use of it is to bring him unto life, unto Christ, that he may live. Tis true, in performing both these offices it acts the part of a severe schoolmaster. It drives us by force, rather than draws us by love. And yet love is the spring of all.[41]

39. Ibid., pp. 360-61.
40. "The Original, Nature, Properties, and Use of the Law," in Outler, ed., *The Works of John Wesley,* vol. 2, p. 15.
41. Ibid.

This description of the law as a "severe schoolmaster" refers to Calvin's understanding of the need for the flesh to undergo "tutelage" and "discipline." But Wesley is obviously uncomfortable with Calvin's "tearing of the flesh" and his emphasis on the law as a "halter to check the raging and otherwise limitlessly ranging lusts of the flesh," so he qualifies Calvin's language by setting the purpose of the law in terms of the love that characterizes the divine life. Wesley's second use — bringing us to life — is much more positive than either Luther's or Calvin's second use — restraining through political coercion.

Wesley's third use of the law is still more positive:

> The third use of the law is to keep us alive. It is the grand means whereby the blessed Spirit prepares the believer for larger communications of the life of God.[42]

Although Wesley is in continuity with Calvin's third use of the law, he far surpasses Calvin in its positive import. He even says that the law of God "is a copy of the eternal mind, a transcript of the divine nature; yea, it is the fairest offspring of the everlasting Father, the brightest efflux of his essential wisdom, the visible beauty of the Most High."[43] This description reveals that Wesley understands the law in Christological terms. It also shows that he understands the third use of the law as a means of sanctifying grace by which we actually participate in the Triune Life. Grace does not merely justify us before the judgment of the law; grace empowers the believer to live the law, and thus the law becomes grace.

Wesley gives an example of this use of the law:

> The law says, "Thou shalt not kill," and hereby (as our Lord teaches) forbids not only outward acts but every unkind

42. Ibid., p. 16.
43. Ibid., p. 10. I am thankful to Ted Campbell for pointing this quote out to me.

word or thought. Now the more I look into this perfect law, the more I feel how far I come short of it; and the more I feel this, the more I feel my need of his blood to atone for all my sin, and of his Spirit to purify my heart, and make me "perfect and entire, lacking nothing."[44]

For Wesley, the law is a means of grace that draws us into the divine life. This is also a description of his theology of discipline. Discipline is restraining and convicting only for those who are still lumbering under their sins. For the redeemed, the discipline of the law is actually gracious.

Wesley's theology of discipline gives a specific shape to the polity of the Methodist Church. The early Methodist movement was a recovery of the importance of discipline. Discipline was the salve that the Spirit applied through the church to heal Christians from sinful self-interest. The healing occurred through the application and interpretation of the General Rules among a small group of Christians. In this small group setting, Christians would discuss the rules to determine ways in which they sinned. The discussion had a stated purpose: "The design of our meeting is to obey that command of God, 'Confess your faults one to another, and pray one for another that ye may be healed'."[45] This healing required the presence of other Christians because of the nature of sin. The sin that takes root in our hearts is often not transparently evident to us. We need others who are willing to speak the truth in love about the state of our soul; for others can often see our self-deception more easily than we can. The purpose of the "Rule" is only to assist in the process of exposing the "mystery of our iniquity."[46]

The mystery of our iniquity is that we would kill God.

44. Ibid., p. 18.

45. "Rules of the Band Societies," in *The Works of John Wesley,* vol. 9, ed. Rupert E. Davies (Nashville: Abingdon Press, 1989), p. 77.

46. "The Mystery of Iniquity" is an important sermon by John Wesley. This subject will be discussed more thoroughly in the next chapter.

That fact alone lends strong support for a pacifist stance for the church. If our sin killed God once, then we should be very cautious about ever taking life again, for fear that we should find ourselves fighting against God when we had assumed we were fighting with God. I do not assume that this argument will compel anyone to a pacifist position, but the great mystery of our iniquity should compel us all to a theology of discipline that will graciously interrogate the ways in which our lives are bound by sin so that sin might be overcome. This is good news; but it is also dangerous and risky news. It requires honest debate and discussion about whether our complicity in violence and warfare contradicts our participation in the salvation brought by Jesus.

CHAPTER FOUR

# Counseling as a Practice of Reconciliation

The salvation that comes to us in Jesus is a salvation that overcomes sin. John Wesley knew this well when he wrote:

> We may learn from hence, in the third place, what is the proper nature of religion, of the religion of Jesus Christ. It is θεραπεία ψυχῆς [therapy of the soul], God's method of healing a soul which is *thus diseased*. Hereby the great Physician of souls applies medicine to heal *this sickness;* to restore human nature, totally corrupted in all its faculties.[1]

Salvation involves the overcoming of the particularities of our spiritual diseases. For some, this means overcoming dishonesty or cowardice. For others, different spiritual diseases need to be overcome. These spiritual diseases are never generic; they always manifest themselves in concrete and particular ways. One can easily overcome sin in general; it is the concrete manifestation of it in our everyday lives to which we tenaciously cling.

One concrete manifestation of our sinfulness is found in our attempt to secure our own existence free from God's creative and redemptive purposes through the use of force, violence, and coercion.[2] This disease is not unique to our genera-

1. "Original Sin," in *The Works of John Wesley,* vol. 2, ed. Albert C. Outler (Nashville: Abingdon Press, 1985), p. 184.
2. God's creative and redemptive purposes are the same; both are

tion, nor is our generation more susceptible to it than any other generation. If there is any universal common to every generation, a major contender would be our inordinate desire to control our own existence and secure our own future rather than accepting the future God offers us in Christ.

## THE MYSTERY OF OUR INIQUITY

We do not naturally know that sin is the attempt to secure our own existence apart from God. We do not naturally know that we are the killers of God. We are taught this frightening truth by the story of our faith, which is exemplified in the flow of the church year. We begin the church year with Advent, a time of preparation when we await the coming of the Messiah. Christ comes, but we always forget who he is. We reduce the Christ child to a sign of God's presence in children and are unable to see the terrifying vision this child brings, a vision that Simeon shows to us in the appointed Gospel lesson for the first Sunday in Christmas:

> Behold, this child is set for the fall
>    and rising of many in Israel,
> and for a sign that is spoken against
>    (and a sword will pierce through your own soul also),
> that thoughts out of many hearts may be revealed.
>                                    (Luke 2:34-35)

Simeon's prophetic gift is not his ability to see God's presence in the birth of children. Rather, it is his ability to see the beauty

---

found in Jesus. For a wonderful account of sin as the attempt to secure our own existence, see Stanley Hauerwas, *The Peaceable Kingdom* (Notre Dame: University of Notre Dame Press, 1983), particularly chap. 3, "On Being Historic: Agency, Character, and Sin."

and terror of the cross in this child. This child is the one who pierces the soul of Mary, and thus the soul of the entire church. He causes many to rise and fall. And he reveals the secret places in our hearts.

Looking at the Christ child, Simeon sees the cross; he sees all of us arrayed against God and crying out, "Crucify him! Crucify him!" To look upon the Christ child without seeing the cross, and without hearing your own voice join in the universal cry against him, is to reduce Christmas to mere sentimentality that is far less threatening than the terrifying vision of Simeon.

However, the terrifying vision of Simeon is difficult to avoid as the church year continues. From Christmas through Epiphany perhaps mere sentimentality is possible, but it becomes far more difficult as we enter into the season of Lent. Lent, much like Advent, is a time of preparation for baptism, which means that we prepare ourselves as a church to be a people who are formed by the death and resurrection of Christ.

While we always forget for whom we wait in Advent, we are given a second chance to remember in Lent. Lent is also a time in which we prepare ourselves to remember who we are. Lent culminates in Good Friday, when we find the secret places in our hearts revealed. We are taught a lesson that penetrates to the depth of our being — "Crucify him! Crucify him!"

We kill God because God threatens us. How can we control our own future and secure our own existence (which is the primary purpose of our present society), how can we be assured of unrestrained freedom of conscience, when we constantly have this meddling God who will not let us be? How can we fulfill the quest for autonomy when we are constantly being reminded that we are only creatures and there is a Creator? So we kill God.

Friedrich Nietzsche understood this better than most theologians. He described it graphically in "The Gay Science":

> "Whither is God" [the madman] cried. "I shall tell you. *We have killed him* — you and I. All of us are his murderers. But

how have we done this? How were we able to drink up the sea? Who gave us the sponge to wipe away the entire horizon? What did we do when we unchained this earth from its sun? Whither is it moving now? . . . Away from all suns? Are we not plunging continually? Backward, sideward, forward, in all directions? Is there any up or down left? Are we not straying as through an infinite nothing? Do we not feel the breath of empty space? Has it not become colder? Is not night and more night coming on all the while? Must not lanterns be lit in the morning? Do we not hear anything yet of the noise of the gravediggers who are burying God? Do we not smell anything yet of God's decomposition? Gods too decompose. God is dead. God remains dead. And we have killed him."[3]

Nietzsche correctly understood that we killed God. He also understood that the death of God let loose new possibilities for the human race. Now we could seek to create our own existence: "Is not the greatness of this deed too great for us? Must not we ourselves become gods simply to seem worthy of it? There has never been a greater deed; and whoever will be born after us — for the sake of this deed he will be part of a higher history than all history hitherto."[4] This is our greatest desire. We want to free ourselves from God so that we can be the makers and controllers of a new history — a history that we write ourselves.

While Nietzsche penetrated into the human heart better than most theologians, he did not have a keen vision into the Triune Life. This separates his revelation of the secret things from that of Simeon. Simeon and Nietzsche both see the horror of our deed, but they define the beauty of it differently. For

3. "The Gay Science," in *The Portable Nietzsche*, ed. Walter Kaufmann (New York: Viking Press, 1954), p. 95.
4. Ibid., p. 96. Of course, Nietzsche also thought that the madman had come too early, and the time for killing God was not yet complete.

Nietzsche, the beauty of it is that now we can create our own gods and create a new history. For Simeon, the beauty of it is that God turns our rebellion back upon us in the resurrection. For Nietzsche, "God remains dead." For Simeon, "The Lord is risen, the Lord is risen indeed, alleluia."

Of course, most of us live our lives gripped by the power of Nietzsche's vision rather than Simeon's. As long as the doctrine of civilization is at the base of Methodist beliefs, with its notion of the supremacy of the individual's freedom to choose, Nietzsche's vision rather than Simeon's holds sway. The hold of Nietzsche's vision on our lives often manifests itself in our warring, where we try to write our own history.

The vision of Simeon does not end with the resurrection. It moves into Pentecost, where the attempt at Babel to construct our own world "and make a name for ourselves" is reversed through the overcoming of divisions of race, language, and nations. The work of the Holy Spirit brings reconciliation and peace. The season of Pentecost reminds us that the Holy Spirit is still present in the life of the church working this reconciliation.

Thus the very flow of the church year reveals God's character to us as well as our own. The revelation of God's character, as well as the revelation of who we are, should be a significant reason for the practice of peace in our life together as a church. Perhaps it does not rule out all participation in war and military service, but it certainly places the burden of proof on those who choose to participate in war rather than on those who refuse to do so.

We have discussed how the church year reveals the secret places in our own hearts and how these secret places are found wanting. This want is caused by our incessant and inordinate desire to make a name for ourselves and free ourselves from God; we are driven by inordinate self-will to secure our own lives. Our will is not yet directed to God's reconciling purposes, and because it is not bound by God's purposes it is not free. Instead, our will is bound to the violence and self-interest of the everyday.

This is the "mystery of our iniquity," the disease of our souls that results in violence and war. Now that we have defined the disease and understood how salvation is a "therapy of the soul," we can turn to discuss Christian participation in war within the context of a theology of discipline.

## THERAPY OF THE SOUL

Up to this point, we have established a theological context within which pastors can counsel parishioners concerning military service and its alternatives. This context is practical divinity, with a theology of discipline as a confessional exercise aiming at holiness of heart and life. This theology assumes that the Spirit uses disciplinary exercises to heal the mystery of our iniquity, which is our attempt to secure our own existence free from God.

I have not yet directly addressed the question of war and peace. There is a reason for this. Too often discussions of war and peace begin by assuming that we can create a typology and offer options or principles from which people can then select. In contrast to this, I wish to surround every discussion of war and peace with a theological discussion of communal discipline, because the language of war should remind Christians of the language of disease.

This chapter will, in fact, develop a typology of various positions on war that have been taken by non-Christians and Christians. But it will do so only by emphasizing penance and reconciliation as the context for the discussion. Most United Methodists are not preoccupied with making appropriate public policy; therefore, if our discussions of war and peace are to be generally accessible, they must do more than address those who make public policy. Every United Methodist should be concerned with repentance and reconciliation, and thus every member of the church should find himself or herself addressed by a discussion of war that focuses on reconciliation as the purpose for the discussion.

Within the United Methodist Church, any discussion of war should take the form of a penitential practice. The purpose of a penitential practice is not to reject and abandon people but to reconcile them. But this reconciliation cannot overlook the violation of the restriction against killing; otherwise we implicitly tell people that no matter what they do, if they do it sincerely it is acceptable. This would abandon all of us to our own idea of sincerity and open the door for incredible self-deceptions. For all of us know that we can see the sins of others much more easily than we can see our own. We need the practice of honestly confessing to one another, risking the intimacy that allows others into our lives to examine our own actions. This examination is the practice of penance, and it is at the center of a theology of discipline.

Wesley realized the importance of the repentance of believers. In a sermon on this subject he distinguished two forms of repentance. He admitted that there was a "repentance and faith" that was "the gate of religion; . . . necessary only at the beginning of our Christian course, when we are setting out in the way of the kingdom." But then he went on to say:

> But notwithstanding this, there is also a repentance and a faith (taking the words in another sense, a sense not quite the same, nor yet entirely different) which are requisite after we have "believed the gospel"; yea, and in every subsequent stage of our Christian course, or we cannot "run the race which is set before us". And this repentance and faith are full as necessary, in order to our continuance and growth in grace, as the former faith and repentance were in order to our entering into the kingdom of God.[5]

5. "The Repentance of Believers," in *The Works of John Wesley*, vol. 1, ed. Albert C. Outler (Nashville: Abingdon Press, 1984), pp. 335-36.

The good news of the gospel is not simply that we are accepted and God affirms us. What kind of good news is that to those of us who know the violence, hatred, sensuality, pride, and slothfulness of our own hearts? The good news of the gospel is not only that God forgives us and pardons our iniquities but also that, through the practice of penance and the power of the Holy Spirit, God intends to overcome the evil that binds us.

> In this sense we are to *repent* after we are justified. And till we do so we can go no farther. For till we are sensible of our disease it admits of no cure. But supposing we do thus repent, then are we called to "believe the gospel". . . . He is able to save you from sins of omission, and to supply whatever is wanting in you. It is true, "This is impossible with man; but with [the] God-man all things are possible." For what can be too hard for him who hath "all power in heaven and in earth"? Indeed his bare power to do this is not a sufficient foundation for our faith that he *will* do it, that he will thus exert his power, unless he hath promised it. But this he has done: he has promised it over and over, in the strongest terms. He has given us these "exceeding great and precious promises," both in the Old and the New Testament. So we read in the law, in the most ancient part of the oracles of God, "The Lord thy God will circumcise thy heart, and the heart of thy seed, to love the Lord thy God with all thy heart and all thy soul." . . .
>
> You have therefore good reason to believe he is not only able but *willing* to do this — to "cleanse you from all your filthiness of flesh and spirit," to "save you from all your uncleannesses." This is the thing which you now long for: this is the faith which you now particularly need, namely, that the great physician, the lover of my soul, is willing to "make me clean."[6]

Salvation is a therapeutic healing of sin, and such healing occurs through the practice of penance.

6. Ibid., pp. 347-48.

Wesley's theology is not new or unique; it is traditional Anglican theology. In Anglican theology, as Kenneth Kirk explains it, the practice of penance has three parts:

1. A virtue (penitence)
2. a discipline (penance proper)
3. a sacrament (absolution as the completion of a good penance).

Corresponding to these three parts are "three stages":

1. Confession
2. Penitential Exercises
3. Reconciliation.[7]

Notice that discipline is never an end in itself; its end lies in reconciliation. Notice also that penance requires the second stage of discipline. Without discipline the reconciliation would be only superficial, because the practice of penitence involves the second type of repentance that Wesley described, a penitential practice that "makes me clean." This cleansing occurs through the application of the third use of the law, in the effort to make one live ever more fully in God.

Wesley's theology of discipline has roots not only in Anglican theology but also in the early medieval period and in the use of books known as penitentials. The penitentials were books that categorized sins and the appropriate penance for each sin so that Christians could be freed from sin.

The seventh-century document known as the "Penitential of Theodore," for example, views theology as therapeutic healing, in a way similar to Wesley. Consider Theodore's interpretation of Jesus' first sermon, found in Matthew 4:17. The RSV translates these words as "Repent, for the kingdom of God is at hand." But Theodore translates them as "because the king-

---

7. Kenneth E. Kirk, *The Vision of God* (London: Longmans, Green, 1943), p. 286.

dom of God is at hand, we can do penance." Penance is not an act of despair, but an act of grace. This understanding of penance is similar to Wesley's second type of repentance. It offers life to those who have been justified. The presence of the kingdom makes possible a true transformation of our character through penance. This is why the preface to the penitential states, "the Lord Jesus, when he was baptized before us all, proclaimed as the instrument of his teaching for those who had no means of healing; saying: 'Do penance.' "[8] Penance provides healing for those who knew no healing.

The connection between Wesley's theology of discipline and medieval theology of penance is not simply conjecture. Wesley himself made this connection. In his sermon "On Laying the Foundation of the New Chapel," he wrote:

> The regularity of [the early Methodists'] behaviour gave occasion to a young gentleman of the college to say, "I think we have got a new set of *Methodists*" — alluding to a set of physicians who began to flourish at Rome about the time of Nero, and continued for several ages. The name was new and quaint; it clave to them immediately. And from that time both those four young gentlemen, and all that had any religious connection with them, were distinguished by the name of "Methodists".[9]

The sect to which Wesley alludes is the same sect from which the theology of the penitentials was derived.[10] Indeed, the very name "Methodists" implies a theology of discipline.

8. John T. McNeill and Helena M. Gamer, eds., *Medieval Handbooks of Penance* (New York: Columbia University Press, 1938), p. 183.

9. "On Laying the Foundation of the New Chapel," in *The Works of John Wesley*, vol. 3, ed. Albert C. Outler (Nashville: Abingdon Press, 1986), p. 581. Wesley had many stories explaining how the name "Methodists" came about, and he would use them as they suited his purpose. See Richard P. Heitzenrater's *Mirror and Memory: Reflections on Early Methodism* (Nashville: Kingswood Press, 1989), for a discussion of this.

10. See McNeill and Gamer, eds., *Medieval Handbooks of Penance,* p. 44.

In the development of the practice of penance, three questions were utilized to assist in discovering the nature of sin:

- What was the purpose of the person in acting?

- What were the circumstances in which the person acted?

- What were the means by which the person acted?[11]

These three questions enabled the confessor and confessee to explore the "mystery of iniquity." Yet these three questions were not meant to destroy. They had a set purpose — "that you may be healed." This purpose for our life together was the reason why "rules" were developed by the church. They provide resources to allow us to know what we need to confess and what disciplines we need to undergo to move from sin to holiness, so that we might experience a true reconciliation.

A theology of discipline requires pastors and other trained persons to utilize the three classic questions of moral theology, as well as the General Rules of our tradition, just as a physician would utilize the diagnostic instruments at her or his disposal. Let me tell you a story to explain my point. A farmer was in his field when he noticed a thief hauling his milk cow away. The milk cow was his only source of food for his newborn child. The farmer yelled at the thief to stop. The thief, startled by the farmer's voice, began to run as fast as he could, pulling the cow behind him. The farmer pursued the thief, picked up a rock, and hurled it. It struck the thief in the head, and the thief died.

What happened in this incident? The first question to ask yourself is why you should be concerned about this at all. On purely consequentialist grounds, you may not be. If all

11. See John Mahoney, *The Making of Moral Theology* (Oxford: Clarendon Press, 1987), p. 180.

that concerns moral reflection is the consequences of actions, then the action is complete and there is no reason to inquire any further. But suppose this farmer happens to be a member of your church, baptized into Christ and therefore dead to the world. Part of your tradition states "Thou shalt not kill." Thus, the ability of your church to witness with integrity is at stake. Therefore you draw upon the "rule" of the church — not to condemn, but to cleanse and effect a reconciliation.

Still, you do not yet know if the church rule has been violated. Here is where the three questions are helpful. The first question to be asked is "What was the purpose of the farmer in acting?" Using the rule of the church as a guide, you seek out the purpose from the person. Vengeance, hatred, the result of an ongoing argument about who was the cow's true owner — all of these would be inappropriate reasons for the action and would violate the integrity of the community. Protection of one's child might be different. The second question to be asked is "What were the circumstances in which the farmer acted?" How large was the rock? Was there a smaller rock nearby? Where did the farmer aim the rock? Could the farmer have merely hit the thief in the leg with the rock instead of in the head? And the third question to be asked is "What were the means by which the farmer acted?" Is there something intrinsically in violation of the rule of the church in throwing a rock at another human being? All of these questions are brought to bear upon the farmer. They are not judgmental and constraining; they are gracious. They provide a way of letting us know the "mystery of iniquity" in our own lives so that we might be enabled to confess our sin truthfully and be cleansed from it, individually and communally, for the sake of our mission to the world.

The purpose of confession and discipline is always reconciliation. Thus the practice of penance cannot stop with the interrogation of the farmer but must include suggestions of disciplines that will enable the farmer to overcome any dis-ordered desires that are discovered. Then the practice is completed with a liturgical celebration of reconciliation.[12]

## COUNSELING CONCERNING CONSCIENTIOUS OBJECTION AS A PENITENTIAL DISCIPLINE

We now turn to resources for fulfilling the *Discipline*'s mandate to counsel parishioners concerning military service and its al-ternatives, bearing in mind that the following discussion of Christian responses to war can only be faithful when its context is practical divinity, penance, discipline, the purpose of holi-ness, and the rule of the church in our communal life, rather than secular notions of pragmatism, freedom of conscience, and civilization.

We are not the first people to live the Christian life. We are not the first people to face questions of war and peace from the perspective of a faithful Christian life-style. Others have gone before us. Our present warring is not so radically distinct from earlier warring that traditional Christian reflection on war must be discarded. No matter what form it has taken — the intentional starting of an epidemic to destroy whole peoples by launching diseased animals into fortified cities with trebu-chet artillery in the Middle Ages, or the slaughter of Native Americans in the "New World," or using the atomic bomb on Nagasaki and Hiroshima — war has always threatened the sur-vival of some aspect of the human species. To assume that our historical situation is so unique that we no longer need to listen to the witness of those who have come before us is the height of human pride.

12. Such a liturgical celebration can be found in the Anglican *Book of Common Prayer*, "The Reconciliation of a Penitent."

Listening to those who went before us, however, does not necessarily mean that we will replicate their behavior. At times we will find their witness woefully inadequate. We will find that they did not live up to their own rule. We may even need to confess and exercise self-discipline because of ways in which we have benefited from their faithless witness. At other times we will find their witness inspiring and wait for the Spirit to create their vision in our own lives.

Theological reflections on war often begin with a typology with three positions — pacifism, just war, and crusade. This typology was developed by Roland Bainton in his *Christian Attitudes Toward War and Peace*. Bainton's book is immensely helpful in describing the beginnings of certain types of positions that he labels pacifism, just war, and crusade, but his three types are too decisively drawn; he fails to see the overlap between the various positions. In addition, the stated reason for his book is the uniqueness of our present historical conjuncture:

> In our time when the atomic bomb threatens to end the atomic era, the ethical problems of war and peace cry urgently for re-examination.[13]

To begin with this assumption is inappropriate for a theology that seeks to live the discipline. By starting with this assumption, rather than seeking to let our lives be transformed through living the discipline, we require the discipline to adjust to something supposedly self-interpreting that is called "our present age." That this would be the case if we follow Bainton's project is clear from his conclusion:

> At the present juncture there is more need for peace than there is for pacifism. If peace is preserved it will be through

13. Roland Bainton, *Christian Attitudes Toward War and Peace: A Historical Survey and Critical Re-evaluation* (Nashville: Abingdon Press, 1988), p. 13.

the efforts not of pacifists, but of peace-minded nonpacifists, who do not renounce war absolutely, but who oppose war in our time on grounds of the humanitarian and the pragmatic.[14]

It is helpful to employ at this point the three questions we examined earlier. What is the purpose of Bainton's pacifism? It is the preservation of the human species. Is this an appropriate purpose within Christian theology? Are we responsible for the preservation of the human species? I think not; this is God's task. What are the circumstances within which Bainton is working? Bainton is motivated by the pragmatic necessity of securing peace in the present historical juncture. Is this a violation of the church's rule? Perhaps not, but it seems to imply that we need to be "culturally relevant" and adjust our discipline accordingly, rather than to live our discipline. What are the means by which Bainton wants us to act? He wants us partially to oppose war on "humanitarian" and "pragmatic" grounds rather than to renounce war absolutely. Does this violate our "rule"? Based on Article 16 of our Confession of Faith, I think so.

Bainton's typology places traditional Christian thinking about war into three types: first, there were the pacifists who refused to participate in war at all; second, there were the just warriors who saw war as a tragic necessity until Christ returns, but who placed great restraints on their participation in war; and third, there were crusaders who fought with no restraints because they believed they were fighting holy wars. On the basis of the three questions that help us ascertain the nature of our acts, you should see that these three positions do not give us enough information to be helpful. Further questions need to be asked — for example, what is the purpose of the actions of the pacifist or warrior? What are the circumstances in which these acts occurred? What are the means by which the pacifist or warrior acts?

14. Ibid., p. 253.

### *The Blank Check and Aggressor-Defender Approaches to War*

John Howard Yoder and Paul Ramsey offer two much more nuanced accounts of the various types of Christian responses to war. Yoder adds a type that he calls the "blank check" to Bainton's three types of positions. The blank check position, according to Yoder, may be the most common position among people in the United States. Yoder defines the blank check position as the willingness to do whatever the ruler asks of us:

> The ruler may for his own purposes be able to explain to himself his reasons, which may be principled, even idealistic, or simply selfish, but the rest of us (the citizen, the journalist, the diplomat, the moralist) have no handles and cannot call him to account.[15]

Thus if the ruler asks us to fight, we do so — assuming that the ruler knows the reason and that we are not responsible to question it.

Ramsey adds another position that he calls the "aggressor-defender" approach. Ramsey believed this position to be the dominant view of war in the United States. Five points characterize this position:

1. *Just occasion.* War is only justified by an overt act of aggression.
2. *Voluntarism.* This assumes that aggressors themselves are not bound to go to war. We assume that all people should think that war is wrong, and therefore anyone who does initiate hostilities does so only because he wills to do something evil.
3. The only reason to go to war is "to banish force from

---

15. John Howard Yoder, *Christian Attitudes to War, Peace, and Revolution: A Companion to Bainton* (Elkhart, IN: Co-op Bookstore, 1983), p. 82.

history." Thus we are always fighting wars to end war and to create a "new world order" (which unfortunately looks a lot like the old world order every time).

4. Because we, as civilized people, only fight when aggrieved, and because the aggressor is morally evil in initiating hostilities and we are fighting for the noble ends of banishing force, therefore "in war military necessity should prevail"; the ends justify the means. We place few restraints on our warring; we do what is necessary to win.

5. Any preventive war is ruled out.[16]

Ramsey, who favored a just war position himself, realized the faithless nature of the aggressor-defender position. It resembles the just war position in some ways, but it has lost all connection with that honorable tradition.

Yoder's "blank check" approach and Paul Ramsey's aggressor-defender approach appear to be typical of how people in the United States think about war. Both of these positions are much more closely related to the crusade type than they are to just war or pacifism. I find the just war position and pacifism to be more faithful to the Christian tradition than the crusade approach. Yet we must not forget that the crusade tradition is part of our heritage.

## The Crusade Approach to War

The crusade actually has some affinity with a theology of discipline. The crusade began as a "pilgrimage" by which one risked one's life to perform a service to the church by delivering the Holy City from the infidels. From this understanding of

---

16. Paul Ramsey, "What Americans Ordinarily Think About Justice in War," in his book *The Just War: Force and Political Responsibility* (Lanham: University Press of America, 1983), pp. 43-60.

"pilgrimage" the church then developed complex military campaigns that eventually gave rise to the Crusades.

I assume that everyone who reads this book will find the crusade type reprehensible. But why exactly are we opposed to the Crusades? On the one hand, we might despise the Crusades because we forget how thoroughly we are involved in crusades even at the present. Yoder's blank check approach and Ramsey's aggressor-defender approach both resemble a crusade type much more than they do any other. Perhaps we despise the Crusades because they are still so much with us. On the other hand, we might despise the Crusades because we see them as bloody battles over religion and because we see ourselves as a "civilized" people who no longer fight over "religion." "Civilized" people, so we think, have overcome such barbarism.

Such a self-understanding is deeply evil. Why should wars over drugs, oil, self-interest, democracy, and so forth be more moral than wars over religion? The problem I find with the Crusades is not that they were fought over "religion," but that the religion they represented was so deceitful. It made God into an arms dealer whose penance did not bring life and reconciliation but death. A sermon by Bernard of Clairvaux, which sought to convince those who needed to do penance to join a crusade, graphically illustrates the deceitful nature of the god responsible for the Crusades:

> Now is the accepted time, the day of abundant salvation. The earth has been shaken; it trembles because the Lord of heaven has begun to lose his land — the land in which, for more than thirty years, he lived as a man amongst men. . . . But now, on account of our sins, the sacrilegious enemies of the cross have begun to show their faces even there; their swords are wreaking havoc in the promised land. . . . What are you doing, you mighty men of valour? What are you doing, you servants of the cross? . . . Is then the arm of the

Lord grown so short that he himself has become powerless to bring salvation and must needs summon us, poor earthly worms that we are, to defend and restore to him his inheritance? Can he not send more than twelve legions of angels . . . and so free his land? Of course there can be no doubt that, should he wish to, he can do this. . . . But I say unto you, the Lord God is testing you. He is looking down upon the sons of men to see if he can find anyone who understands and grieves over what is now happening on earth. . . . See then with what skill he plans your salvation and be amazed. . . . He is not trying to bring you down but to raise you up. What is it but a unique and wonderful act of divine generosity when the Almighty God treats murderers, thieves, adulterers, perjurors, and criminals of all kinds as though they were men of righteousness and worthy to be called to his service. Do not hesitate. God is good. . . . He pretends to be in debt so that he can repay those who take up arms on his behalf with the forgiveness of sins and with eternal glory. . . . I would call blessed that generation that has the chance to obtain so rich an indulgence, blessed to be alive in this year of jubilee, this year so pleasing to the Lord. . . . O mighty soldier, O man of war, you now have a cause for which you can fight without endangering your soul; a cause in which to win is glorious and for which to die is but gain.[17]

In light of this call to discipline, we can understand why people became alarmed at a theology of discipline and gradually neglected it. The three movements themselves — confession, penitential exercises, and reconciliation — cannot stand alone. They only make sense when they are firmly rooted in Jesus. Jesus' life, teachings, death, and resurrection do not point to some generic type of reconciliation, but to a specific kind of reconciliation that includes the cross and suffering.

17. Cited in Hans Eberhard Mayer, *The Crusades,* 2nd ed. (Oxford: Oxford University Press, 1988), pp. 96-97.

Suffering love, not the infliction of violence, describes the reconciliation between the Trinity and the world accomplished in Jesus.

The reconciliation that comes about through killing the infidels is not our reconciliation; it is false. We know that it is false because it does not destroy the root of violence in the soul of the believer but only further accentuates it. The falseness of this reconciliation is depicted by the deceiving and mischievous god Bernard depicts in order to sanction the killing. This god "tests" the crusaders and "pretends to be in debt." This god could "send more than twelve legions of angels . . . and so free his land," but instead he gives others the chance to do his killing for him. And their killing becomes their salvation. The infliction of violence rather than suffering love defines this false salvation. Bernard's god is vicious, spiteful, deceitful, and bloodthirsty. Such a god is not worthy of worship.

This bloodthirsty god resembles the Norse god Thor much more than the divine Trinity. Of course, most of us are more comfortable worshiping the warrior god Thor than the Trinity. We understand Thor because we are so much like him. But for Christians, the divine Trinity can be understood only through the second Person — the Son. We do not know God until we have heard about the Son. The Son is not simply one manifestation of God among many, nor is he just one mode of God's existence among other modes. He expresses the inner life of God, which has been present from before the creation of the world. The Trinity is a central Christian doctrine for us because it allows us to know who God is.

God is found in Jesus. Therefore, the vision we find in Jesus, primarily attested to in Scripture and in the worship life of the church, establishes the context within which the three movements of confession, penitential exercises, and reconciliation fit. Once this is recognized, then we also see that the crusade model, the aggressor-defender type, and the blank check position do not fit. They are contrary to the purpose of our reconciliation; they do not create suffering love, but the infliction of violence. They are to be avoided.

Does this then mean that we must be pacifists? Not necessarily, but we should notice that even in Bernard's call to join in the Crusade a restriction against war is presupposed. Bernard tells the would-be soldiers that because of the unique nature of this war, "you can fight without endangering your soul." The obvious implication is that Bernard realized that killing in war does "endanger the soul" of Christians. Thus, something like a crusade was necessary to overcome this prohibition.

Yet the prohibition against killing within the Christian tradition was not first loosened by a crusade; a prior and more faithful loosening of the prohibition occurred in another response to war that is known as "just war theory." Unlike the crusade, the just war position does seek to take seriously the call to suffering love.

### The Just War Approach

In distinguishing the crusade type from the just war type, I am overlooking an important historical point — namely, that people who fought in crusades described their actions in terms of just war theory. Only after the fact did people affix the term "crusades" to their actions. Hans Eberhard Mayer states, "Not until the mid-thirteenth century was there a Latin word for 'crusade' and even then it was seldom used." People who fought in the Crusades imagined themselves to be fighting in a just war because they believed their cause to be a just one.[18] "Just cause" was only one of the criteria for "just war." Yet in the Crusades, people assumed that if the cause were just, then all the effective means necessary should be employed. In this

18. Mayer, *The Crusades*, pp. 14-15.

116

sense, the crusade and Ramsey's notion of "aggressor-defender" warfare are quite similar.

The fact that crusade and just war are not very easily distinguishable should make us wary of any typology that seeks to make clear distinctions between them. There is no action in history that fits nicely into any typology. There is no single thing we can call a just war over against a crusade — or even over against pacifism. Life is simply too messy and complicated for such nice distinctions. For the practice of discipline, the distinctions can be helpful in leading people into new possibilities. Where people have imagined themselves to be just warriors, it is beneficial to show them that they are actually crusaders or aggressor-defenders. Still, the typology by itself will not be all that helpful; more is needed to accomplish the necessary reconciliation.

The "more" that is necessary is the habituation of peaceable virtues by a community committed to holiness of heart and life, and willing to be bound together by a common discipline to accomplish this purpose. Remember that this is the theology we developed before we began any discussion of various approaches to war. Even though we are now discussing the development and complexity of both just war theory and pacifism, this "more" must not be forgotten.

Just war theory is not unique to Christianity. Pagans, such as our forebears the Greeks and the Romans, had a doctrine of just war long before it was incorporated into the moral life of the Christian church.[19] In the Christian church, St. Ambrose, who drew upon the work of the pagan Cicero, is given credit for first developing a Christian just war theory, and St. Augustine is most often put forward as providing the first sustained development of just war.

Why did these Christians incorporate a just war position? The argument goes like this. For the most part, in the first three

19. See Cicero *De officiis* 1.10-13.

centuries Christians were pacifist.[20] This pacifist stance was understood primarily as opposition to idolatry. To serve in the military required worshiping other gods. (Perhaps it still does!) In the fourth century, Constantine, the emperor of Rome, realized the political expediency of Christianity and therefore converted. In so doing he unified his empire, and people in the military were actually required to be Christians. At this time, the just war doctrine made its appearance in the Christian church.

The appearance of the just war doctrine is interpreted in two ways. Influential theologians such as Troeltsch and Harnack have interpreted it as the church coming of age and realizing that it must take "responsibility" for the world at large. Lesser-known theologians such as Cadoux have interpreted it as a time of apostasy when the church refused to be responsible to the gospel and instead opted for a safer life.

Wesley interpreted the age of Constantine as a "fall." He wrote:

> Persecution never did, never could give any lasting wound to genuine Christianity. But the greatest it ever received, the grand blow which was struck at the very root of that humble, gentle, patient love, which is the fulfilling of the Christian law, the whole essence of true religion, was struck in the fourth century by Constantine the Great, when he called himself a Christian, and poured in a flood of riches, honours, and power upon the Christians, more especially upon the clergy.

Wesley thought that the Constantinian shift had so contaminated the church that "The few Christians that are upon the earth are only to be found where you never look for them."[21]

---

20. See C. John Cadoux, *The Early Christian Attitude to War* (New York: Seabury Press, 1982), and Adolph von Harnack, *Militia Christi: The Christian Religion and the Military in the First Three Centuries*, trans. David McInnes Gracie (Philadelphia: Fortress Press, 1981).

21. "The Mystery of Iniquity," in Outler, ed., *The Works of John Wesley*,

The interpretation of the Constantinian shift is a central debating point between those who believe that the gospel requires Christians not to go to war and those who believe that the gospel requires Christians to go to war (with certain restrictions) in responsible defense of the neighbor. Some who believe in a just war position interpret the Constantinian shift as the church being thrust into a role of greater responsibility. For them, the move from pre-Constantine to post-Constantine Christianity did not strike at the heart of the Christian faith because the same thing that had compelled Christians not to fight now compelled them to fight — the fulfillment of the second part of the Great Commandment: "Love your neighbor as yourself."[22]

Obviously, one of the problems with justifying war on the basis of "love for neighbor" is the problem of self-deception. We deceive ourselves into thinking that what we are doing is "loving our neighbor" by destroying an enemy, but actually we wreak vengeance upon an enemy who is still our neighbor. This potential self-deception has eternal consequences for Christians. Souls could be lost if people deceive themselves and cultivate hatred and violence rather than faith, hope, love, and peace because of the permission to participate in war. Thus the church developed categories by which the actions of people who participate in war are to be assessed. Christians who fight cannot participate in an unjust war, or participate in a just war unjustly. The categories, which together define the just war position, interrogate our motives; without any such criteria we

vol. 2, pp. 463 and 465. I am indebted to my friend Clinton Spence for this quote. He pointed out this wonderful sermon to me.

22. See Paul Ramsey's *War and the Christian Conscience* (Durham, NC: Duke University Press, 1961), pp. xv-xxiv, for an interpretation of Constantine that does not see discontinuity between Constantinian and pre-Constantinian Christianity. For a different view, see John Howard Yoder's "If Christ Is Truly Lord," in his book *The Original Revolution* (Scottsdale, PA: Herald Press, 1977), pp. 52-84.

simply legitimate our activity on the basis of our own preference and subjectivity, and we will not know when we are deceiving ourselves and putting at risk the witness of the church.

Just war theory is a witness by those who have gone before us on the journey of faith about how they handled the difficult problem of the relationship between faithful Christian discipleship and war. As it is formulated today, just war theory is divided into two sets of criteria. The first set refers to just reasons that can require or permit Christians to go to war. The second set refers to how Christians must act once they are in a war. Within each set of criteria many different positions have been held within Christian tradition.

### The Justice Necessary to Go to War

*1. Just Cause*   What constitutes a good reason to go to war? In developing just war theory, theologians had to overcome two decisive claims of Christian discipleship. First, Christians had been baptized into the death and resurrection of Christ. If they had been so baptized, how could they now refuse death and take up arms against someone? Second, how could they kill others and not violate the great commandment of love for God and neighbor? Only when a neighbor is threatened and in need of defense can Christians even begin to think about using violence against others. Self-defense and self-interest are never faithful reasons for Christian use of violence. For this reason, the National Conference of Catholic bishops defines just cause in this way:

> War is permissible only to confront "a real and certain danger," i.e., to protect innocent life, to preserve conditions necessary for decent human existence, and to secure basic human rights.[23]

23. National Conference of Catholic Bishops, *The Challenge of Peace: God's Promise and Our Response* (Washington: United States Catholic Conference, 1983), p. 28.

The gospel imperative to love our neighbor disallows war for reasons other than when our neighbor is threatened.

2. *Competent Authority*  Who is competent to declare war? This is a problematic and controversial category. The Catholic bishops' pastoral interprets competent authority to mean that "war must be declared by those with responsibility for public order, not by private groups or individuals." However, this interpretation is more indebted to the Dutch canonist Hugo Grotius and the development of international law than to an understanding of just war as defense of neighbor.

Grotius reversed the understanding of competent authority of an earlier theologian named Franciscus de Victoria. Victoria suggested that the prince alone was not competent to declare war: "one must not undertake war on the sole advice of the King, nor on the advice of a few people, but only on the advice of a number of wise and honest citizens."[24] Grotius rejected this notion. He wrote:

> Franciscus Victoria allows the inhabitants of a town to take up arms . . . to redress their own wrongs, which the Prince neglects to avenge, but such an opinion is justly rejected by others.[25]

John Calvin held a position between those of Grotius and Victoria. He disagreed that the ruler alone should issue the call to take up arms. Instead, he wrote:

> I am so far from forbidding [lesser magistrates] to withstand, in accordance with their duty, the fierce licentiousness of kings, that if they wink at kings who violently fall upon and

24. Franciscus de Victoria, "Lessons on the Right of War," par. 60-68, in Maurice Barbier's translation (Geneva: Libraire Droz, 1966).

25. Hugo Grotius, *The Rights of War and Peace* (Westport, CT: Hyperion Press, 1979), book 1, chap. 3, p. 58.

assault the lowly and common folk, I declare that their dis--
simulation involves nefarious perfidy, because they dishon-
estly betray the freedom of the people, of which they know
that they have been appointed protectors by God's ordi-
nance.[26]

For Victoria, any group of "wise and honest citizens" constituted competent authority. Grotius conceded this authority
only to the sovereign ruler. Calvin did not allow any group of
citizens to initiate hostilities, nor did he confine authority to
the ruler alone, but he allowed "lesser magistrates" justly to
initiate acts of warfare. Thus a great diversity exists within
Christian tradition concerning who constitutes competent authority.

All of these views of competent authority were developed
under political conditions different from the nation-state system within which we live. How should we who are Christians
in the United States understand what constitutes competent
authority? Is the president alone the competent authority? Is a
vote of Congress necessary for Christians to fulfill the just war
criteria? Because the criterion of competent authority was developed in a time when ecclesial authority and civic authority
were closely identified, should we not take competent authority
to mean a competent ecclesial authority such as bishops, synod,
assembly, conference, etc.?

3. *Comparative Justice*　The criterion of comparative justice asks
which side is "right." Some just war theorists argue that one of
the criteria for fighting is that "our" side must have a compara-
tively more just cause than the other side. This can be a problematic criterion because it can allow us to justify aggressor-
defender warfare. Because we believe we have a more just
cause, we fight for unlimited goals. But unlimited and uncon-

26. John Calvin, *Institutes of the Christian Religion,* ed. John T. McNeill
(Philadelphia: Westminster Press, 1960), 4.20, vol. 2, p. 1519.

ditional warfare is outside the pale of Christian responses to war. According to just war criteria, Christians can only fight to redress particular wrongs. Christians can never fight for unconditional, abstract values such as "to make the world a safer place" or "to construct a new moral order." To fight for reasons such as these is a type of atheism; Christians believe that only God brings his kingdom. At most, we can only participate in what God is doing by invitation.

While some just war theorists argue that Christians can only fight when their side is comparably more just, other just war theorists such as Paul Ramsey and Victoria argue that "our side" need not be comparably more just. Both sides can have an equal claim for justice and this is all that is required for a just war. This is an attempt to recognize the tragic nature of our lives in the time before the kingdom is completely consummated. We always fight for limited ends, and thus while our side might be just, the other side could have an equal claim to justice.

*4. Right Intention*  With what attitude does one fight? Soldiers must fight with an intention congruent with just cause. They can harbor no hate for the enemy. If they hate the enemy, they endanger their souls and the witness of the church. Soldiers must understand that while what they do might be "necessary," it does not allow them to forget the claims of discipleship on their lives.

How do we assess "intention"? We all know that our intentions are often mixed and the mixed elements cannot be easily separated. The just war criteria are rules by which intention is assessed. Just war theory follows the same three movements as theology of discipline. The intention must be congruent with the purpose for which all of our discipline exists, and that is reconciliation as defined in the peace of Christ. If this is not the intention of the soldier, then the soldier fights unjustly and endangers his or her soul. Therefore, the task of the confessor is to heal soldiers of the hatred that is often

123

inculcated in them by those who encourage them to war. Such hatred will destroy their body and soul.

5. *Last Resort* Is war a faithful alternative? Last resort asks only if "all peaceful alternatives have been exhausted." Many pacifists use "last resort" as a way to critique just war. When war breaks out they argue that we had not yet reached the point of "last resort." Unfortunately such arguments often under-write an aggressor-defender concept. The hidden assumption is that until the enemy is actually on our shores, raping and pillaging our people, resort to war is not yet justified. But that is not the true point of last resort.

Last resort occurs when no peaceful way exists to protect the innocent. If you are going to accept just war reasoning, then you have to understand the relationship between just cause and last resort. Once actual hostilities have broken out, or once the "competent authority" has been convinced that they will break out, then we are at the stage of "last resort." Then the duty to protect the innocent takes over and "last resort" is no longer relevant.

Complete economic embargoes are unacceptable on just war grounds. They are indiscriminate, and (as we shall soon see) discrimination is a necessary criterion for just war. There-fore, "giving the sanctions time to work" is not necessary for last resort. In fact, asking government leaders "to give sanctions time to work," when the sanctions are part of a complete em-bargo, violates just war theory.

6. *Probability of Success* Are we likely to win the war? This criterion separates Christian just war theory from classical, pagan theories. It requires that — even if your cause is just — if you have no hope of success, then you must sacrifice your land, your government, etc., rather than fight a hopeless battle.

Probability of success could be an immoral criterion except for the claim of Christian discipleship upon our lives. The reason for this criterion is that it is better for us to live and bear witness to the gospel than to maintain our possessions, our government, and so forth. Defeat in battle may be a way in which God brings people who have not heard the gospel to us so that we can evangelize them. Such is the "good news" for an elect people!

For pagans, war is a matter of "honor." Honor must be upheld. If your cause is just, then it does not matter whether you can win or not. You must fight to the death — even if you sacrifice all of your people.

In challenging the pagan notion of war, we must be careful not to become "Machiavellian." That is to say, we must not calculate the consequences of our participation in war only from the perspective of self-interest. That also violates just war criteria. As the Catholic bishops remind us, the purpose of the "probability of success" criterion is "to prevent irrational resort to force or hopeless resistance when the outcome of either will clearly be disproportionate or futile." Humility is a Christian virtue; honor is not.

7. *Proportionality* This is a straightforward criterion. "The damage to be inflicted and the costs incurred by war must be proportionate to the good expected by taking up arms."[27] Proportionality applies both to "our" side and to "theirs." You cannot seek to inflict more damage to an enemy than the enemy himself created. If the enemy has seized a portion of land and you think the enemy has done that unjustly, then your purpose is to right a wrong, not to punish or destroy the enemy. Thus your actions must be proportional to the just cause.

*       *       *

The above seven criteria explain the reasons for which Christians can legitimately go to war. They are not to be applied in

27. *The Challenge of Peace*, p. 31.

a rigid, deductive fashion; they are to be used skillfully by theologians, pastors, and laity to help explain how we can all move through confession to discipline and reach reconciliation. Two other criteria remain to be discussed. These are the criteria by which Christians must act when they participate in war.

### The Justice Necessary by Which One Fights in War

1. *Discrimination* This principle states that only those directly involved in the war can be the focus of a Christian's attack. Because the legitimation for Christian participation in war is protection of an aggrieved neighbor, means cannot be used by which you yourself become an aggressor against other neighbors.

Only those people who are directly engaged in war are legitimate combatants. To kill others directly and intentionally is not war but murder. Thus the bombing of Nagasaki and Hiroshima, the firebombing of Dresden, and the indiscriminate firefighting in Panama (which directly killed a large number of civilians) are, by just war criteria, not acts of war but of murder. Murder is ruled out for Christians.

One objection to the principle of discrimination is that in modern warfare everyone is a combatant. That of course is not true. To take an example from recent history, one of the things that most incensed us during the Gulf War was the fact that Iraq launched indiscriminate attacks on Israel that had no military usefulness. Such actions offend us so deeply because of our residual commitment to the principle of discrimination. The amazing thing is that we use the principle of discrimination against the other side, but refuse to apply it to ourselves. Thus in a news interview Defense Secretary Dick Cheney affirmed Truman's decision to bomb Hiroshima and Nagasaki because it brought a quicker end to World War II.[28] Whether Cheney

28. "This Week With David Brinkley," Feb. 3, 1991.

and Truman were correct in that assessment is beside the point. In Christian just war theory, murder is always ruled out, even if it means you lose more of your own troops than you would have otherwise. The structure of Cheney's argument is no different from Saddam Hussein's. Both assume that through a violation of the principle of discrimination they can secure more of their own troops and thus bring a successful completion to the war.

The principle of discrimination is the most difficult and the most important aspect of just war. We need to ask ourselves what kind of fidelity, courage, and commitment are necessary for a people to live by this principle. If we are unable to live by the principle of discrimination, we should no longer call our wars just, and we should certainly hesitate in taking upon ourselves the name Christian.

2. *Proportionality*   We have already mentioned proportionality as a criterion for going to war; it also qualifies the way in which Christians can participate in war. The way in which the war is conducted must not exceed the purpose for which the war is fought. If your reason for going to war is to free the people of Kuwait, then you cannot destroy Iraq. That is clearly disproportionate on just war grounds. As a matter of fact, if your reason for going to war is to free the people of Kuwait, then you cannot even destroy Kuwait. What kind of "liberation" is it which leaves nothing to be liberated? Destruction is vengeance, and vengeance is not our task.

\*       \*       \*

The just war criteria are important as a witness to us from past believers who sought to take seriously Jesus' claims upon their lives while at the same time confronting the tragic and deep injustice of our earthly pilgrimage. If war is necessary for Christians, then the just war criteria must be upheld as the way in which wars are to be fought. This means that we may have to be open to surrender. Just war theory does not assume that you fight according to these criteria unless the enemy refuses to do so; you fight like this because it is just. If we are not going to fight in this way, then we should admit that our wars are unfaithful and call them aggressor-defender warfare or crusades or admit that we are taking a "blank check" approach; but let us at least have enough respect for those who have gone before us in the faith to assume that they took these criteria seriously and to allow them to be a judgment upon us.

All of the just war criteria require interpretation. In the hands of a skilled but faithless or immoral casuist, they can be used to justify nearly anything.[29] Thus the context for the use of these criteria must always be the reconciliation that comes to us from the faithful and obedient life, teachings, death, and resurrection of Jesus.

In the preceding discussion of just war, I have attempted to be as gracious as possible to a position with which I disagree. I find just war problematic because I am convinced that our understanding of just war today has to do with the attempt to construct just war as a natural law that serves the power of the state (drawing on the work of Grotius), rather than understanding just war as a penitential practice (drawing upon the work of Victoria). Augustine, to whom the genesis of just war is often attributed, was not attempting to make public policy or international law. His understanding of just war, like Victoria's, confronted a pastoral, churchly problem. What do you do with those people who violate the rule of the gospel and kill their neighbors? For Augustine, just war theory was a penitential discipline that sought to reconcile people back into the church. But with Grotius the nature of just war changed; it lost its

29. See John Howard Yoder's *When War is Unjust: Being Honest in Just War Thinking* (Minneapolis: Augsburg Publishing House, 1984).

connection with the theology of discipline and became a positive duty that assists the power of the state. The latter view I find unacceptable for faithful Christian discipleship. The former I find helpful for pastoral ministry.

## Pacifist Approaches to War

I find a pacifist stance most appropriate as a faithful witness to the gospel within the tradition of United Methodism. If this were only my personal opinion, you would be free simply to discard it. However, I think it is something more than that. The United Methodist Confession of Faith, the Holy Scriptures, and the tradition of the church all lead me to the conviction that we should all seek to be transformed by the Spirit into this peaceable people. Lest you think my language here suggests that war is appropriate until we are transformed, let me be clear. I am not making the claim that we participate in violence in the present and violate who we will be when we are transformed. We struggle even now, refusing to participate in violence, realizing that this refusal is necessary but insufficient. Our peaceableness is not complete until our prayer, worship, and activity participate fully in the life of Jesus' obedience to the Father in the power of the Holy Spirit. Perhaps that only happens after death; or perhaps, as Wesley thought, it can occur in this life. Either way, our lack of complete participation in God's peaceableness does not give us permission to wage war in the present. We seek to become who we will be, knowing that this transformation can come about only through grace and not through our own efforts.

Thus the pacifism to which I am ascribing is a specific type of pacifism, a pacifism that is consciously a part of our participation in the life of the Trinity. The Trinity is the peaceable, social presence of God with God's self, and it is our gift to be privileged — through the life of Jesus — to participate in that peaceable, social presence.

"Pacifism," like just war theory, is not a single stance; there are many kinds of descriptions and interpretations of pacifism. Some of the descriptions we find are faithless and should be shunned. Others may have some affinity with a Christian pacifism and can be affirmed. But the reader must realize that "pacifism" does not invoke just one position. In a little book entitled *Nevertheless,* John Howard Yoder highlights eighteen different descriptions of pacifism. For the sake of brevity, I will examine only five.[30]

## 1. Cowardly Pacifism

This is a pacifism that is based on the notion of self-preservation. Nothing is more important than my own life. Life is an end in itself, and my life must be preserved at all costs. This type of pacifism is found in liberal contract theories of government — the kind we find in our own constitution.

The United States' toleration of conscientious objectors is largely due to this understanding of political government.[31] Government is a matter of each individual submitting his or her will to the will of the majority. Because government is a matter of a voluntary contract where my life is best preserved through offering my will to another, the government cannot ask me to lose myself by fighting.

30. John Howard Yoder, *Nevertheless* (Scottsdale, PA: Herald Press, 1971). This is not an attempt to distill Yoder's discussion into five categories. A lot is left out here, just as Yoder himself admits that a lot is left out in his eighteen types. I would encourage anyone interested in this topic to read Yoder's book for a fuller presentation.

31. It also has to do with the attempt to accommodate the historic peace churches, but this accommodation is not because the U.S. government thinks their position is correct but because of its own understanding of politics.

The political theorist Thomas Hobbes allowed for conscientious objection on the basis of government as a voluntary association. He wrote:

> [A] man that is commanded as a soldier to fight against the enemy, though his sovereign have right enough to punish his refusal with death, may nevertheless in many cases refuse, without injustice; as when he substituteth a sufficient soldier in his place: for in this case he deserteth not the service of the commonwealth. . . . When armies fight, there is on one side or both, a running away; yet when they do it not out of treachery, but fear, they are not esteemed to do it unjustly, but dishonourably. For the same reason, to avoid battle, is not injustice, but cowardice.[32]

Hobbes allows for refusal to participate in war because of cowardice. Everyone should fight, but because government is a voluntary organization, everyone cannot be forced to fight; otherwise the basis upon which government is structured would be violated.

An exception to this right of conscientious objection occurs when the government itself is threatened with extinction. Because the only way to secure freedom is by submitting your will to the government, if the government is jeopardized, freedom would be lost. Therefore, when freedom itself is threatened, the government has the right to force people to fight.

If political government is understood in liberal democratic terms, then conscientious objection can only be understood as cowardice. This is quite common, and it is the reason why many people say that while they object to people who oppose the state's prosecution of war, they will defend their right to express their opinion. Such a statement only marginalizes the voice of those pacifists by refusing to hear their witness.

32. Thomas Hobbes, *Leviathan* (London: Fount Paperbacks, 1983), p. 211.

It patronizingly suggests to them that their position is only possible because other people are willing to kill for them. Thus it assumes they are cowards.

Yet being a pacifist or a conscientious objector in a world at war may take great courage. Your state, possibly your family, and unfortunately even your church might brand you as a cowardly and immoral person. You can go to jail or be exiled for such a position. You can be placed on the front lines as a medic. Standing against war takes courage. In fact, refusing to question a government's right to use you to kill other people could actually be the cowardly act.

Liberal political theory falsely assumes that the type of government we currently have is necessary for "freedom." This is an intolerable position for Christians. For us, freedom is not dependent upon any particular government. Freedom is defined by being bound to Christ. The main function of government is to secure the possibility of the free preaching of the gospel. This means that the government must allow us freely to call people not to participate in faithless acts of the government. Neither legal, nor moral, nor any other type of pressure should hinder the free preaching of the gospel.

Cowardly pacifism is not a faithful option for Christians. People who accept that true political government is a matter of submitting their will to the government on a contractual basis and who understand that submission and government as necessary for "freedom" should not be legally accepted as conscientious objectors, because their only rationale for pacifism is cowardice. They no longer desire to submit their will to the majority because their own life will be threatened. That this type of pacifism is present in our society is true without a doubt, but it is not the only type. Other forms of pacifism that are rooted in following Jesus are also present.

## 2. Pacifism as a Political Strategy

The pacifism we noted in Chapter 2, expressed in such statements as the 1908 Episcopal Address of the Methodist Episcopal Church, was a pacifism deeply indebted to a Kantian theory of the state that held that the inevitable progress of civilization required pacifism. Pacifism was seen as an effective political strategy to make the world a better place. This is a naive pacifism that refuses to take seriously the sinful nature of our world. When pacifism did not work as an effective national strategy, we saw a shift in 1944 within the official stance of the Methodist Church from a pacifism that would make the world safe for democracy to a crusade position that would use violence to make the world safe for democracy. The theology for both of these positions remained the same. The essence of Christianity was found in democratic structures that denoted an inevitable moral progress, culminating in freedom of individual conscience. The purpose of Christianity was to apply this essence to culture and transform it. If peace did not accomplish this, then violence was necessary.

Pacifism may or may not be an effective political strategy, but that is a secondary concern. Our first concern is whether or not pacifism is the most appropriate response to the claim of discipleship on our lives, a claim that comes to us from the life, teachings, death, and resurrection of Jesus. Pacifism does not guarantee that the world will be a safer place. Pacifism may very well get us killed. In fact, pacifism may require that we allow others to die for our convictions. But that is nothing new; warfare also asks others to die for our convictions. Pacifists refuse to inflict that violence, even if it means that they allow others to suffer by their refusal.

Pacifism as a political strategy lacks any firm rootage in Christian tradition. I see nothing distinct about it that would lead me to think that other grounds, such as Kant's moral philosophy, would not provide as satisfactory a moral base for this position as would Christianity. A distinctively Christian position requires a form of peace witness that is different from seeing pacifism as an effective political strategy.

### 3. Sectarian or Vocational Pacifism

One way to be consistently pacifist would be to accept the claim that pacifism could never be politically responsible, so pacifists should remove themselves from all acquaintance with the government and be sectarian. In this view pacifism is a vocation for only a few enlightened people, while all the rest are left with the difficult task of living in a world where political choices are not easily made. This is a purist pacifism that seeks isolation. Few pacifists actually ever claim that this is what they are doing. But this sectarian type of pacifism is often used against pacifists by those who believe that force must sometimes be used because of our responsibility to care for others.

Perhaps some pacifists do understand themselves to be a-political. If that is the case, then I find this position difficult to accept. But most pacifists are not a-political; they simply assume that a single political order or government cannot ensure freedom. They see themselves as alternative political orders that could potentially be imposed on the whole world. Christian pacifists cannot be a-political, for we are to go into all the world and proclaim the gospel. Thus we cannot isolate ourselves from the world by accepting a sectarian option.

### 4. Principled Pacifism

What do you do with those statements in Scripture that seem to posit absolute restrictions against killing? Principled pacifism abstracts a single principle from Scripture — for example, the commandment "You shall not kill" (Exod. 20:13) — and uses it as a theological base. What requirements does this pose on Christians? If one understands the law and the gospel as contrary, then the "law" can easily be dismissed as no longer relevant. But this, as we discussed in Chapter 3, is inappropriate for theologians who want to work in the Wesleyan tradition. The law is gracious. It brings not only judgment but also life. "You shall not kill" is not a negative and restrictive claim, but a positive one — you need no longer kill because God's covenant provides new possibilities for you.

We cannot dismiss this commandment simply because the Hebrew word for "to kill" may have the more restricted meaning of "to slay" or "to murder." The covenant does not lead us to ask how we can interpret Scripture in the most limited way possible; rather, we are to ask what God is doing that will allow us to participate most fully in God's redemptive purposes.

Another Scriptural passage that the principled pacifist draws upon is the Sermon on the Mount:

> You have heard that it was said, "An eye for an eye and a tooth for a tooth." But I say to you, Do not resist one who is evil. But if any one strikes you on the right cheek, turn to him the other also; and if any one would sue you and take your coat, let him have your cloak as well; and if any one forces you to go one mile, go with him two miles. Give to him who begs from you, and do not refuse him who would borrow from you.
>
> You have heard that it was said, "You shall love your neighbor and hate your enemy." But I say to you, Love your enemies and pray for those who persecute you, so that you may be sons of your Father who is in heaven; for he makes his sun rise on the evil and on the good, and sends rain on the just and on the unjust. (Matt. 5:38-45)

The principled pacifist does not begin, like most of us, by asking how we can avoid this difficult teaching. Instead, the principled pacifist finds in these words a revealed principle that is to be lived. The question is not, "How can we make this passage relevant to a world where turning the other cheek is a dangerous thing to do?" The question is, "How can my life become relevant to this Scripture?" The principled pacifist position has the advantage of taking Scripture seriously.

I find this position attractive and more faithful than the first three positions mentioned. However, it can have the disadvantage of developing single principles apart from the context of Jesus' entire life and the ongoing life of the church. Simply holding to a single principle pulled from Scripture is insufficient. Other teachings in Scripture — when they are abstracted from the story of Christ's obedience, life, teaching, death, and resurrection — could be used to offer other absolute positions that would be in direct contradiction to this one. For instance, Paul's statement on obeying government authorities in Romans 13 could become the source of a principle that says that Christians are always to obey their governments no matter what they are asked to do. That of course does not fit with the whole story of Jesus' life or Paul's. Paul spent a great deal of his life in prison. And even the act of the resurrection, as Daniel Berrigan reminds us, was "illegal." The tomb was sealed and guarded; it was illegal for anyone to open the tomb, and yet this is precisely what God did. Still, if we are going to abstract a principle from the story and make it an absolute in defense of pacifism, separate from the story of Jesus, then we should grant the same privilege to those who do the same for war. For this reason, I do not find the principled pacifist position convincing. Because it turns Scripture into an absolute principle, it makes the issue of pacifism a proscription against killing rather than an expression of a people's faithfulness and participation in God's redemptive purpose.

### 5. Virtuous Pacifism

Peaceableness is, first and foremost, a virtue reflecting the inner life of the Trinity. The Trinity's work of salvation for us claims us for participation in the Triune Life. Because the Triune Life is peaceable, our salvation enables us, through that participation, to be a peaceable people. Thus, pacifism is not a cowardly vice, nor primarily a political strategy, nor a withdrawal from the real world, nor an implication drawn from revealed absolute principles that we are to achieve in our own strength; pacifism is a virtue the Spirit works in us as we participate in the obedience of the Son in the unity of the Trinity.

Virtuous pacifism requires the distinctiveness of the cultivating presence of the Spirit. We are part of a community where swords are beaten into ploughshares, and where those ploughshares are used to cultivate peace in our lives. Such cultivation occurs in our worship life. Through worship, the church gathers as a new people "out of every nation, tribe, tongue and people" (Rev. 5:9). This suggests that we are not bound merely by geographical boundaries; thus, such boundaries cannot provide an intelligible reason for us to war. The sacrament of baptism into the death and resurrection of Christ marks us as a new people who have already accepted Christ's victory over our death and who anticipate the presence of the peaceable kingdom above all other kingdoms. Our confession of sin and the forgiveness we receive remind us that there is a resource for healing the violence in our souls. The proclamation of the Word invites us to participate in Jesus' obedience — an obedience that refused to secure his own life but offered himself for us all. In the peace and reconciliation we experience before the Eucharist, as well as in the Eucharist itself, we participate in that obedience. And then we are sent out into the world to be a people of service and witness to the whole world.

Virtuous pacifism is not based on an absolute principle that is defensible for all people in all times and places. Rather, it draws upon the story of our redemption in Jesus and says that the best way to live as people who have experienced this redemption is by refusing to kill, even in times of war. It draws upon the resources at our disposal as United Methodist Christians to make an argument about a difficult case of conscience. That is the best we can do. Virtuous pacifism seeks only a casuistical analysis of the reasons for war in which the theological reasons are primary. Thus virtuous pacifism draws on the Methodist tradition of practical divinity.

# Conclusion:
## One More Unfinished Agenda

This book has been an exercise in practical divinity, making an argument for peace as a "virtuous pacifism." The argument for pacifism, I am convinced, is the most faithful way of articulating United Methodist responses to war. Using the "rule" of the church — Article 16 of our Confession of Faith and paragraph 439.i in our *Book of Discipline* — we seek to cultivate the holy temper of peaceableness through practical divinity.

I hope the argument in this book will be used as a "rule" by which the community of faith practices holiness. I realize that an argument based on these sources is a rather risky foundation on which to make such a radical commitment as pacifism requires. Still, I believe this is all we have — a faith that seeks understanding but can never fully seize understanding. Many questions remain unanswered. The task of any member of the United Methodist Church, or of any reader who is not United Methodist but who has a sisterly or brotherly concern for our faithfulness, is to tell my story better, for it is a story that belongs to all the baptized.

Three things remain to be done. First, I want to convince you that the argument presented in this book has broader implications than simply counseling concerning military service and its alternatives. War only highlights an aspect of our sinful rebellion that is manifested in a myriad of other ways. Second, the clergy have been charged to counsel not only members of

139

the church but also *the wider community.* Thus knowledge of the laws surrounding conscientious objection, as well as resources for further knowledge, will assist in fulfilling the rule of the church. Third, in good practical divinity fashion, I will conclude with the story of a friend who has made some tremendous sacrifices in her effort to be faithful to Christ's call on her life.

## THE GRAVEYARD BATTLE

War is an exceptional situation for moral analysis. It is not a normal part of our lives; that is why we give it a special name — *war.* But the faithless attempt to secure our own existence *is* a part of our everyday lives. To combat this disease by concentrating only on the exceptional situation is poor medicinal practice. Therefore, let me draw upon an everyday example of parish ministry to illustrate how our discussion about Christian participation in war has broader implications for pastoral care.

Several years ago, I served in a typical church in a typical rural setting. The church was composed of three main families, and the history of the church could be told by which former pastors each of the families invited back to participate in family occasions such as marriages, funerals, and family gatherings. The pastor was a visible sign of a time when a particular family had gained ascendency in the parish, exercising control over church affairs — and usually over the other families. When the former pastor returned to participate in a family occasion, the family would reminisce about battles lost and won and accomplishments achieved during his reign. Each family sought to broaden the church beyond the parochial borders that were erected (each family supposed) by the previous family's reign. Usually the "broadening of the parochial borders" meant including, in some capacity, friends and family of the ruling family.

During my pastorate, the family that had gained ascendency were good friends of George, who lived next to the church. Some years before, George had donated a parcel of land to the church for graveyard space. Graveyard space was a precious commodity for us. We had little land, and the graveyard had steadily grown until we no longer had a place for the youth to play touch football on Sunday afternoon. George's contribution had placed him in good stead with our people.

George now faced a post-mid-life crisis. He realized he was on the downside of life and, not being a churchgoer, he was uncertain where his final resting place would be. George approached the patriarch of the reigning family, knowing full well that he, rather than the pastor, held the power in the church. George asked for assurance that a plot of land would be given him on the day of his inevitable demise. Like a good Methodist, the patriarch of the church called a meeting of the committee on burial and grounds (not to be confused with the committee on funeral preparations, which was not nearly as prestigious) and asked them to give George assurance that his request would be honored.

When George's request was brought before the committee for approval, I assumed that we would automatically accept his request. Much to my surprise, one wonderfully cantankerous woman objected on the grounds that George had never been to our church, he was not baptized in our church, he did not get married in our church, and giving money to the church was an insufficient reason to be given a plot of ground for burial. After all, only limited space was available, and we needed to be cautious with the space we had. What I thought would be a perfunctory yes turned into concerted resistance. And that was only the beginning.

The two subordinate families began to realize that the ascendent family's power was not only over present churchly life but even over the life to come. With limited graveyard space, no one could be assured that all of her or his familial relations would be buried next to each other. My phone began to ring. "If George is to be given the spot south of the oak tree which faces his property, my family and I want assurance that we can have the five plots north of the large rock." The phone continued to ring, and after a time we all realized that more plots were desired than the land could hold.

To solve the problem we called another meeting of the burial and grounds committee. We decided to handle the problem *administratively*. We developed a map of the graveyard, sectioned it into various plots, and developed a system whereby each family could justly place its request for space.

Handling this situation administratively was an extraordinary act of cowardice on all our parts. For the problem was not just limited space in the graveyard; the problem was a spiritual disease: we did not trust each other. We feared that others would use the last earthly act performed upon our bodies as the ultimate exercise of power over us. Since we did not trust each other, we had to develop a system of justice by which we could avoid submitting our lives to each other. This kind of "justice" is only necessary when peace and reconciliation are absent.

The problem of the graveyard battle was a particular manifestation of our attempt to secure our own existence by avoiding the submission of our lives to other people. This is a concrete sickness that needs the "therapy of the soul." To seek to solve the problem administratively was cowardly, but we found this to be the least divisive way to "manage" the situation and maintain order — order, but not peace.

If the ministry is understood only in terms of management and maintaining order, the graveyard battle was handled successfully. If the ministry is understood as providing therapy for the soul, patterned after the vision of Jesus, the graveyard battle was handled poorly. The peace and reconciliation brought by Christ are not merely "order." In fact, they often upset the order. Rather than seeking to manage churches and constantly put out fires, we sometimes need to allow the Holy

Spirit to stoke up the embers and allow the flames to consume us.

The mandate to counsel concerning military service and its alternatives does not mean creating appropriate public policy in order to engineer a peaceable world through our own efforts. Such a purely intellectual virtue cannot be found within Christian morality. This counseling is to be a therapy to heal our disease of a warlike spirit, whether that warlike spirit manifests itself in explicit acts of military violence or in administrative council meetings. The mandate to counsel begins with seeing and understanding the sin in our lives, and realizing that Christ overcomes our sin and allows us to do so also. To begin with the question of "war" in the abstract, without realizing that what makes war questionable for us is the same sinful daily reality that makes us battle over graveyard space, is to possess the form of Christian morality without its content.

The desire to secure our own six feet of land free from all other people's control is the same desire that causes us to secure territory from other nations for our own self-interest. It is also the same desire that causes us to kill God to secure our own life free from God. To confess the sin of one of these desires requires confessing the sin of the others. To allow that desire to have free rein in our lives is to construe the world on the basis of Nietzsche's vision: "Must not we ourselves become gods simply to seem worthy of such a deed?" But we are not God; we are not responsible for securing our own lives, the life of a nation, or the life of the human species. We are created; we are dust, and to dust we shall return. Learn this lesson, and you will see why the mandate to counsel concerning military service and its alternatives is not different from the mandate "To administer the Sacraments of Baptism and the Lord's Supper and all the other means of grace." It is part of our witness to the world that God is present, reconciling the world to God's self.

## WITNESSING TO THE WIDER COMMUNITY, USING THE NATION'S LAW

Our discussion of the *Discipline*'s mandate to counsel concerning military service and its alternatives has been restricted up to this point to our theological tradition. Still, the mandate requires pastors to counsel members of the church "and the community." The wider community is important. Counseling concerning military service and its alternatives is a witness to the wider community that we are a peaceable people. In order to witness effectively, an understanding of draft legislation is helpful. Therefore, let me briefly mention the legal possibilities within the United States for conscientious objectors.

Two forms of conscientious objection are possible: one is for those who are not in the military; the other is for those who are already serving in the military.

### *Non-Military Conscientious Objection*

Conscientious objection counseling is not simply a way to allow people to avoid the draft. It is a means of evangelism. It should confront people theologically with why they would or would not participate in war. The process requires people to put a file together that offers a testimonial to their own pacifist commitments. This is a time for people to examine themselves and the beliefs of their church.

Throughout the 1980s the United States military recruited approximately 400,000 people annually to maintain its troop strength, which is second only to China.[1] As long as these numbers can be sustained through a voluntary army, the mil-

1. This information comes from the *Handbook for Conscientious Objectors*, which was developed by NISBCO and can be purchased by requesting it from NISBCO, 1601 Connecticut Ave., N.S., Suite 750, Wash-

itary prefers volunteers. However, in time of war, political leaders often want a draft because it generalizes the burden of war among the population.

Since Vietnam, the draft legislation has drastically changed. Of course, at present the United States does not have a draft, and therefore you cannot legally be a non-military "conscientious objector." There is nothing to object to. Still, new draft laws have been drawn up, registration has been implemented, and if the need for a draft developed Congress could pass the legislation after debate.

The new draft laws provide as little as ten days from the time a person receives a letter of induction to the time when the person would be required to report for service. It is during this ten-day period that any petition for exemption or post-ponement must be filed. Student deferments are no longer possible. Students would be allowed to finish the semester, but then they would be required to report.

Because of the new draft legislation, the only time to file for conscientious objection status if a draft would actually be implemented is during the ten days from which a person re-ceives an induction letter to the time they are to report. This does not offer much time, and most people have not thought through the issue sufficiently to do otherwise than what is expected. Thus conscientious objection counseling should occur before a draft is actually implemented.

People who do find themselves opposed to all war can develop a file for conscientious objection. They can begin creat-ing a file as early as their registration by writing on their reg-istration card that they are "pacifist" and making a copy of their card. This photocopy should be kept in a safe place, because it shows that the person was pacifist before the person was actu-ally drafted. The next step is to sit down with someone and

---

ington, D.C. 20009. The General Board of Church and Society also provides pastors with information concerning conscientious objection.

articulate in writing why the person is a pacifist. This is a good occasion to use the penitential practices outlined in Chapter 3. Then the person should acquire three letters of reference stating that the person's description of his or her pacifist commitments is true.

All of these materials should be kept in a file. The file can be preserved in the local church, but the materials should also be sent away. They can be sent either to NISBCO or to the General Board of Church and Society of the United Methodist Church (which maintains files for conscientious objectors). As well as offering people the occasion to struggle with the question of participation in war, this practice assists conscientious objectors if the draft is reinstated. They will already have the substance of their claim documented.

## Military Conscientious Objection

People in the military can also file for conscientious objection status, but this is a much more complicated and risky process. If a member of the military seeks counseling from you, a sympathetic lawyer who has experience in this field should be found. In fact, a good pastoral practice is to seek such a person out from your wider community and discuss this issue with her or him. The basic reasons acceptable for objectors' status remain the same whether a person is military or non-military.

In counseling conscientious objectors, pastors and others should begin by asking the person if he or she objects to participation in *all* wars. Only those who object to all participation in war are granted conscientious objection status. Thus a just war position is excluded because *selective* conscientious objection is not legally permitted in the United States. Selective conscientious objection means that although a person is not opposed to all forms of war, he or she cannot fight in this particular war because it does not conform to the just war criteria (or some other criteria).[2]

Still, people who are currently in the military can file for conscientious objector status, even though this is a much more complicated process. Military officials, as well as many military chaplains, discourage this practice. While military personnel can legally file, whether or not the military will honor their applications and grant them conscientious objector status is another matter. Our local committee for conscientious objection sent three people to Germany to counsel soldiers who did not want to go and fight in the Gulf War. Many soldiers were opposed to fighting because they thought this war was unjust. Several of the soldiers these people counseled were Christians. One young man had a pentecostal experience and came to the revelation that carrying a gun and following Jesus were incompatible. He filed for conscientious objector status but his application was not received by the military. The church was silent.

Counseling both military and non-military persons concerning how they can claim conscientious objector status requires familiarity with the law of the land and some basic training. This training can be had in a day through NISBCO or the Central Committee for Conscientious Objection. The Board of Church and Society in each annual conference should also be equipped to offer this information to pastors in their conferences. In fact, paragraph 439.i of our *Discipline* mandates it.

Another crucial group in need of counseling are members of the Reserve Officers' Training Corps (ROTC). One month before the Gulf War began, the ROTC took out a full-page advertisement in the Duke University school paper. Half of the page was a picture of a check for $2750.00 that said, "For academic excellence." The rest of the advertisement read:

---

2. During Vietnam, selective conscientious objection was ruled against in the Gillette case. See *The Handbook for Conscientious Objectors*, p. 64.

**YOUR UNCLE WANTS TO PAY FOR COLLEGE.**
**BUT ONLY IF YOU'RE GOOD ENOUGH**

Army ROTC offers qualified students two-year and three-year scholarships that pay for tuition and required educational fees and provide an allowance for textbooks and supplies.

You'll also receive up to a $1000 grant each school year the scholarship is in effect. So find out today if you qualify.

**ARMY ROTC**
**THE SMARTEST COLLEGE**
**COURSE YOU CAN TAKE**

This advertising is greatly misleading. Nowhere does it suggest that ROTC might lead you actually to kill people. ROTC entices our young people to join up for an education. What they volunteer for is "the smartest college course you can take."

Through conscientious objection counseling, members of the armed forces can come to a greater awareness of their faith and realize the incompatibility between following Jesus and using the armed services as a way to pay for a college education. Recently, on Duke University's campus, a member of the Air Force ROTC realized the incompatibility of the two and decided to file for conscientious objector status. She has now put a file together and has given me permission to share her story with you.

## DEFINING HOLINESS:
## THE STORY OF A FAITHFUL FRIEND

When Andrea S. Gansle filed for conscientious objection, the military asked for "a description of the nature of the belief that requires the applicant to seek separation from the military service or assignment to noncombatant training and duty for reasons of conscience." Andrea answered this question by juxtaposing two claims, the first from Jesus, the second from "The Code of the U.S. Air Force":

> "You shall love the Lord your God with all your heart, and with all your soul, and with all your mind. This is the great and first commandment. And a second is like it, You shall love your neighbor as yourself. On these two commandments depend all the law and the prophets."
>
> Jesus Christ, the New Testament (Matt. 22:37-40)

> The Code of the Air Force is a standard of life. . . . Patriotism as practiced in the Air Force is an intelligent devotion to the interests of the United States *above every other consideration.* (original emphasis)
>
> The Code of the U.S. Air Force

Andrea came to the conviction that these two "standards of life" were incompatible and that she could no longer live by the code of the U.S. Air Force.

Let me quote her own testimony to her faith:

> Just as I cannot reconcile these two passages, I cannot reconcile their greater implications. That is to say, I can no longer serve both God and the United States Air Force. The above words of Christ have dramatically and irreversibly altered my life.
>
> Since infancy I have been a Roman Catholic and I have seen and heard this passage from the Bible many times. And

yet, I have never experienced the enormous impact of these words until now. Truly, these words have come alive for me in the past several months, as have all the teachings of Jesus. Christ Himself has ceased to represent merely an impossible ideal; He is, in fact, the very powerful, very real guiding force of my life. I am quite certain that Jesus Christ is the Son of God, and that His commandments must be followed by all those who wish to belong to Him and His Kingdom.

Before I matured in my faith, loving God above all else meant simply trying to be a good person. I loved God by going to church, unless I did not want to. I gave money to the poor, unless I felt I needed it more. I did not place undue emphasis on material possessions, unless I really wanted something. I was kind to others, unless they disappointed or frustrated me. This is what I thought it meant to be a follower of Christ.

Now all that has changed. Now I am committed to dedicating my life to Christ and truly following God's commandments. The first commandment, loving God *above all else,* means precisely that. Therefore, obedience to God is more crucial than acquiescence to earthly authorities. Concerns of material wealth, interpersonal relationships, and the approval of others are subordinated to concerns of devoting one's life to Christ. The second commandment of Jesus is to love others as you love yourself. There are no exceptions to this commandment. I suspect Christ knew how very difficult it would be for His followers to fully accept this particular challenge, and how very easy it would be for us to rationalize contrary behavior. Thus, Jesus clarifies the meaning of this teaching by expressly stating that we are to love even our enemies. For me to follow Jesus' commandments, it is impermissible to remain a member of an organization that takes part in death and destruction of other human beings.

Presumably, many people feel that under certain circumstances armed conflict is the only available alternative for a nation's defense. While I once agreed with this position, I now vehemently disagree. I am convinced that war in any form is absolutely evil and contrary to the will and teachings of Christ. Evil can only be battled and overcome by Jesus' peace and love, never hatred and violence. Granted, throughout the ages, at any given time, a nation or people is threatened. That nation may be deceived into believing that war is the only viable solution. But the use of violence inevitably results in a spiral of escalating hatred and misery. The nation engaging in war will sooner or later rue its actions and suffer irreparable damage.

Visions of world peace resulting from armed conflict, such as the League of Nations, the United Nations, or the "New World Order" have always been and will always remain an illusion of tragic proportion. For if the human race could achieve peace by means of war, surely by now all mankind would live in uninterrupted and blissful tranquility. Regardless of how noble the objectives, a war will always lead to our eventual doom by contributing to the spirit of hatred and destruction. I firmly believe that war, any war, will tear a nation apart in ways that we have not yet begun to imagine.

My beliefs spring from the fact that I fully accept the teachings of Christ and the command that in order to live with God we must imitate the life of Christ. Jesus did not resort to violence to prevent His own torture and murder. He did not hate, nor did He kill. By the standards of modern society, killing His adversaries would have been condoned as an appropriate use of self-defense under the circumstances. But Jesus' conduct does not conform to our current attitudes or standards. Instead of injuring His attackers, He met the horrifying circumstances of His death with a loving and forgiving heart. As Christians, we are to live this teaching to the best of our ability. My dedication to living Christ's peacefulness has truly changed me, and has become a part of my moral code.

I firmly believe that I am called to witness my Christian faith; I embrace Christianity and have made it the foundation of my life. Jesus Christ is truly my savior, and I am determined to repay Him to the best of my ability. I will follow

151

the commandments and teachings of God, and for me this means that I am no longer able to implicitly condone any war by remaining a member of the armed services. Instead, I am called to accept Christ's peace, and to share it with others.

Andrea's witness requires that she accept great risks of alienation from many who do not understand why she refuses to remain a member of the Air Force. But surely those of us who have been baptized and who have felt the pulling of the Spirit to an ever fuller participation in the Triune Life do understand. Because we know what she is speaking about, we should not be a church that merely "tolerates" her witness; rather, we should make it normative and invite others to follow the peaceable Savior.

Is the United Methodist Church pacifist? This question cannot be answered theoretically. Only United Methodists themselves can finally provide the answer by refusing to participate in war. Such refusal is a gift from God that will strengthen our church. May we be strengthened to receive such a gift and to offer it to the church universal in cooperation with the historic peace churches, and may God raise up people who will provide a vision of holiness to cultivate in us the virtue of peace.

# Bibliography

Althaus, Paul. *The Theology of Martin Luther.* Philadelphia: Fortress Press, 1966.

Aquinas, Thomas. *Summa Theologica.* Westminster, MD: Christian Classics, 1948.

Bainton, Roland. *Christian Attitudes Toward War and Peace: A Historical Survey and Critical Re-evaluation.* Nashville: Abingdon Press, 1988.

Behney, J. Bruce, and Paul H. Eller. *The History of the Evangelical United Brethren Church.* Nashville: Abingdon Press, 1979.

Bowne, Borden Parker. *The Atonement.* New York: Eaton and Mains, 1900.

———. *The Immanence of God.* Boston: Houghton Mifflin, 1905.

———. *Personalism.* Boston: Houghton Mifflin, 1908.

———. *The Principles of Ethics.* New York: Harper and Brothers, 1896.

Brown, Robert McAfee, ed. *The Essential Reinhold Niebuhr.* New Haven: Yale University Press, 1986.

Cadoux, C. John. *The Early Christian Attitude to War.* New York: Seabury Press, 1982.

Calvin, John. *Institutes of the Christian Religion.* 2 vols. Ed. John T. McNeill. Philadelphia: Westminster Press, 1960.

Cicero. *De officiis.* Cambridge, MA: Harvard University Press, 1990.

Davies, Rupert E., ed. *The Methodist Societies, History, Nature and*

*Design.* Vol. 9 of *The Works of John Wesley.* Nashville: Abingdon Press, 1989.

Duecker, R. Sheldon. *Tensions in the Connection.* Nashville: Abingdon Press, 1983.

Foucault, Michel. *Discipline and Punish.* Trans. Alan Sheridan. New York: Vintage Books, 1979.

Grotius, Hugo. *The Rights of War and Peace.* Westport, CT: Hyperion Press, 1979.

Harnack, Adolph von. *Militia Christi: The Christian Religion and the Military in the First Three Centuries.* Trans. David McInnes Gracie. Philadelphia: Fortress Press, 1981.

———. *What Is Christianity?* Trans. Thomas Bailey Saunders. Gloucester, MA: Peter Smith, 1978.

Hauerwas, Stanley. *The Peaceable Kingdom.* Notre Dame: University of Notre Dame Press, 1983.

Heitzenrater, Richard P. *Mirror and Memory: Reflections on Early Methodism.* Nashville: Kingswood Press, 1989.

Hobbes, Thomas. *Leviathan.* London: Fount Paperbacks, 1983.

Jansen, Albert T., and Stephen Toulmin. *The Abuse of Casuistry.* Berkeley: University of California Press, 1988.

Kant, Immanuel. *Eternal Peace.* In *The Philosophy of Kant.* Ed. Carl J. Friedrich. New York: Modern Library, 1949.

Kaufmann, Walter, ed. *The Portable Nietzsche.* New York: Viking Press, 1954.

Kirk, Kenneth E. *The Vision of God.* London: Longmans, Green, 1943.

Knudsen, A. C. *The Doctrine of God.* New York: Abingdon–Cokesbury Press, 1930.

———. *The Philosophy of Personalism.* Boston: Boston University Press, 1949.

———. *The Philosophy of War and Peace.* New York: Abingdon–Cokesbury, 1947.

Langford, Thomas A., ed. *Doctrine and Theology in the United Methodist Church.* Nashville: Abingdon Press, 1991.

————. *Practical Divinity: Theology in the Wesleyan Tradition.* Nashville: Abingdon Press, 1983.

————. *Wesleyan Theology: A Sourcebook.* Durham, NC: Labyrinth Press, 1984.

McAdoo, H. R. *The Structure of Caroline Moral Theology.* London: Longmans, Green, 1949.

MacIntyre, Alasdair. *After Virtue: A Study in Moral Theory.* 2nd ed. Notre Dame: University of Notre Dame Press, 1984.

McNeill, John T., and Helena M. Gamer, eds. *Medieval Handbooks of Penance.* New York: Columbia University Press, 1938.

Mahoney, John. *The Making of Moral Theology.* Oxford: Clarendon Press, 1987.

Mayer, Hans Eberhard. *The Crusades.* 2nd ed. Oxford: Oxford University Press, 1988.

Milbank, John. *Theology and Social Theory: Beyond Secular Reason.* Cambridge, MA: Basil Blackwell, 1990.

Minus, Paul. *Walter Rauschenbusch: American Reformer.* New York: Macmillan, 1988.

Monk, Robert C. *John Wesley: His Puritan Heritage.* Nashville: Abingdon Press, 1966.

Outler, Albert C., ed. *Sermons.* Vols. 1-4 of *The Works of John Wesley.* Nashville: Abingdon Press, 1984-87.

Perkins, William. *A Discourse on Conscience and the Whole Treatise of Cases of Conscience.* Niewkoop B. De Graaf, 1988.

Ramsey, Paul. *The Just War.* Lanham: University Press of America, 1983.

————. *War and the Christian Conscience.* Durham, NC: Duke University Press, 1961.

Rauschenbusch, Walter. *Christianizing the Social Order.* New York: Macmillan, 1912.

Schaller, Lyle. *It's a Different World.* Nashville: Abingdon Press, 1987.

Schmid, Heinrich, ed. *The Doctrinal Theology of the Evangelical Lutheran Church.* Trans. Charles A. Hay and Henry E.

Jacobs. Philadelphia: United Lutheran Publishing House, 1899.

Taylor, Jeremy. *Ductor Dubitantium*. London: J. L. for L. Meredith, 1660.

————. *The Rule and Exercise of Holy Dying*. 1651; New York: D. Appleton, 1849.

————. *The Rule and Exercise of Holy Living*. 1650; New York: D. Appleton, 1849.

Tuell, Jack M. *The Organization of the United Methodist Church*. Nashville: Abingdon Press, 1985.

Victoria, Franciscus de. *Lecons sur les Indiens et sur le droit de guerre*. Trans. Maurice Barbier, O.P. Geneva: Libraire Droz, 1966.

Ward, Reginald W., and Richard P. Heitzenrater, eds. *Journals and Diaries I*. Vol. 18 of *The Works of John Wesley*. Nashville: Abingdon Press, 1988.

Wesley, John, ed. *The Christian Library*. Bristol: William Pine, 1768.

————. *Sunday Service of the Methodists of North America*. The United Methodist Publishing House and the United Methodist Board of Higher Education and Ministry, 1984.

Williams, Raymond. *Keywords*. New York: Oxford University Press, 1983.

Yoder, John Howard. *Christian Attitudes to War, Peace, and Revolution: A Companion to Bainton*. Elkhart, IN: Co-op Bookstore, 1983.

————. *Nevertheless*. Scottsdale, PA: Herald Press, 1971.

————. *The Original Revolution*. Scottsdale, PA: Herald Press, 1977.

————. *The Politics of Jesus*. Grand Rapids: Eerdmans, 1972.

————. *When War Is Unjust: Being Honest in Just War Thinking*. Minneapolis: Augsburg Publishing House, 1984.

# Index